D0481797

1964
b x 2/05. 2/07
744/11 8/11

CROSS-
FUNCTIONAL
TEAMS

Glenn M. Parker

CROSS-FUNCTIONAL TEAMS

Working with Allies, Enemies, and Other Strangers

Jossey-Bass Publishers · San Francisco

Substantial discounts on bulk quantities of Jossey-Bass books are available to corporations, professional associations, and other organizations. For details and discount information, contact the special sales department at Jossey-Bass Inc., Publishers. (415) 433-1740; Fax (415) 433-0499.

For sales outside the United States, please contact your local Simon & Schuster International Office.

Library of Congress Cataloging-in-Publication Data

Parker, Glenn M., date.
    Cross-functional teams : working with allies, enemies, and other strangers / Glenn M. Parker. — 1st ed.
       p.   cm. — (The Jossey-Bass management series)
    Includes bibliographical references and index.
    ISBN 1-55542-609-3
    1. Work groups.   2. Intergroup relations.   3. Interorganizational relations.   4. Complex organizations.   I. Title.   II. Series.
HD66.P345   1994
658.4'02—dc20
                                                93-48674
                                              CIP

FIRST EDITION
HB Printing   10 9 8 7 6 5 4 3   *Code 9445*

The Jossey-Bass Management Series

To my father, Melville Parker

C O N T E N T S

Part Three: Toward Cross-Functional Teams

Tools for Developing Cross-Functional Teams

P R E F A C E

A new form of teamwork is quietly becoming a key factor in many of America's most successful and competitive organizations. And it is making for some strange bedfellows.

Research scientists are meeting with marketing professionals; design engineers are working with purchasing department staff; cost accountants are teaming up with operations managers; and computer programmers and office managers are serving together on systems development teams. In many organizations, eight or more disciplines are working together on cross-functional teams to bring a new product to the marketplace, develop a next-generation computer system, design a new layout for a factory floor, produce an important new drug, engineer a complex telecommunications network, prepare a long-term corporate strategy, or implement a procedure to upgrade service quality in a government agency.

As more and more organizations see the potential value

of such teams, the need for clear, specific advice and tangible examples becomes apparent. It is now evident that cross-functional teams are different from and require different approaches than traditional functional teams. While many standard team-building practices are applicable to cross-functional teams, the keys to success lie in the extent to which the organization provides the requisite supports for teamwork.

As cross-functional teams increase in number, we need to know how to make them successful. We need to know how to form the teams, what type of leadership is necessary, what type of training is required, and what procedures in the organization need to be changed or added. We need specific examples from successful organizations, and we need to know what has worked and what has failed.

It will also be important to know what we can borrow from classic team building and apply to cross-functional team building. *Cross-Functional Teams* provides specific advice and practical answers for executives, managers, team leaders, and human resource professionals.

BACKGROUND AND PURPOSE OF THE BOOK

Cross-Functional Teams provides specific advice and practical help for people in organizations who have decided that cross-functional teams are going to be an important factor in their business strategy. I hope the book will also convince others of the value of such teams and will give them the courage to begin the process of incorporating these teams into their day-to-day business operations.

The book had its genesis in questions posed by clients, workshop participants, and audience members at conference presentations. The questions reflected the frustration of people who believed in the concept of cross-functional teams but did not know

- How to get off on the right foot
- How to select a leader
- How to select team members
- How many should be on a team
- What type of training the team should receive
- What to do about performance appraisal
- What to do about compensation
- How to incorporate team rewards and recognition
- How to interface with the functional organizations
- What the role of top management should be

The data that form the basis of this book come from a survey I did of public and private organizations. Before conducting the survey, I searched the literature and my networks to find organizations that seemed to be in the forefront of cross-functional teamwork. (As a consultant and speaker, I have a great opportunity to travel and meet people who are developing leading-edge practices.) I then mailed the survey to the organizations I had targeted and to the top one hundred companies on the 1992 *Fortune* list of America's most admired corporations. I also conducted telephone and face-to-face interviews with people who had worked with cross-functional teams. The purpose of the survey was to find answers to the above questions, and perhaps to others I had not yet thought of. In the end, I was looking for a catalogue of "best practices" that would inspire and help others who are struggling with the potential of cross-functional teams.

AUDIENCE

I wrote *Cross-Functional Teams* with practitioners in mind — executives and high-level managers who are trying to create the right vision and cultural supports; team leaders who are

struggling with the twin goals of getting a job done and keeping a diverse group of people moving toward that end; managers who are wondering how to handle all these people in their
organization who are constantly running off to team meetings;
and human resource professionals who are being asked to
provide training and help others manage this new phenomenon, the cross-functional team.

The most consistent comment I received about my earlier book *Team Players and Teamwork* was that it was both
practical and readable. This is my goal for *Cross-Functional
Teams*, because I know that practitioners want strategies they
can realistically apply to their work environment. This book
will answer questions and provide strategies for a varied
audience:

- Executives and high-level managers in the private
and public sectors are looking for ways to create an organization that encourages and supports cross-functional teamwork.
They want to know what type of message they should send,
what type of direction they should provide, and in what ways
they should change their organization to fit this new direction.
Cross-Functional Teams offers recommendations drawn from
the lessons of other successful organizations. Senior managers
will be especially interested in the chapters on the challenges
faced by cross-functional teams, on team empowerment, and
of course, on management's role in building a team-based
organization.

- Leaders of cross-functional teams will find that many
of the issues they are dealing with are not dissimilar to those
leaders face in other organizations. This book will describe
approaches that have worked and should be tried and those
which are sure to fail. Team leaders will want to pay special
attention to the chapters on team leadership, team empowerment, team goals, team size, and the team working together.

- Midlevel managers and supervisors who are trying to
figure out how to manage people in a team-based organization
will find answers here. With many of their people spending an
increasing amount of time on teams directed by others, the
challenge is how to manage the work, time, and performance

of their subordinates—while getting their own work done. *Cross-Functional Teams* discusses procedures that seem to be working. Particularly relevant will be the chapters on performance appraisal, building bridges, and management's role.

- Human resource professionals will find much of value here. They will be able to use the Survey of Cross-Functional Teamwork at the end of the book to understand teams in their own organizations. They will also be able to apply ideas from the chapter on team learning to training people for cross-functional teams. In addition, they will learn about organizational interventions that other professionals have used to facilitate successful teamwork. The chapters on rewarding teamwork and on team learning will be of special interest.

- Students of organizational behavior and human resource development will find the book a valuable resource for course curricula and research. As cross-functional teamwork becomes a widespread corporate strategy, the academic community will look to this book for answers from the business world. Students will find Chapter One, which provides numerous examples of cross-functional teams, and Chapter Two, which describes the team landscape, and Chapter Three, which outlines the obstacles faced by cross-functional teams, to be useful introductions to the area.

OVERVIEW
OF THE CONTENTS

Cross-Functional Teams begins with a discussion of the six competitive advantages that cross-functional teams provide for an organization. With examples from more than twenty organizations, I show how cross-functional teams are helping to speed up the product development process, improve customer focus, increase the creative capacity of the organization, provide a forum for organizational learning, and serve as a single point of contact for customers, suppliers, and other key stakeholders.

Chapter Two looks at the new teams as they exist in organizations today. Here I describe the various types of teams, including functional, self-directed, and of course, cross-functional teams.

In Chapter Three, I discuss the challenges of cross-functional teamwork. Specifically, I outline the obstacles to success. I explain the various factors that can bring a team down, such as ineffective leadership; unclear authority; ambiguous goals; poor boundary management; performance appraisal that overlooks teamwork; lack of rewards and recognition; interpersonal problems; too many people on a team; and lack of management support.

In Chapter Four, I tackle the key role of team leadership. I show how the leadership requirements of a cross-functional team are different from and more difficult than those of a functional team. I outline the unique characteristics of a successful cross-functional team leader.

Chapter Five describes the issue of team empowerment. Using business examples, I show how empowered cross-functional teams get things done better and faster. Then I discuss how empowered teams get empowered, including what the team can do and what top management can do to encourage empowerment. Finally, I describe a continuum of cross-functional team empowerment and make the point that not all cross-functional teams are or need to be fully empowered.

Chapter Six focuses on team goals. While goal setting is critical to all teams, it is especially important for cross-functional teams. In this chapter, I make the point that clear goals reduce conflicts and encourage the building of partnerships. I also describe the process of setting goals for a cross-functional team, including a clarification of the terms *vision, mission, goals, objectives,* and *action plans.*

In Chapter Seven, I focus on the need for cross-functional teams to build bridges to key stakeholders inside and sometimes outside the organization. I describe the key stakeholders, the inherent barriers to relationships with them, and strategies for building effective interteam relationships.

Chapter Eight addresses the sticky issue of performance appraisal. I look at the need to incorporate performance on cross-functional teams into the organization's appraisal process, and I discuss how some companies are currently doing this. I also describe the concept of team appraisals where members of cross-functional teams are evaluated by other members of their team.

In Chapter Nine, I try to boil down some of the best ideas on how to reward cross-functional teamwork. I provide a smorgasbord of reward programs, such as gainsharing, responsibility-based pay, bonuses, cost reduction programs, revenue enhancement programs, team incentives, recognition programs, and informal recognition. Using the experience of other organizations, I offer specific advice for organizations that want to begin or revise a program to reward cross-functional teamwork.

Cross-functional team learning is highlighted in Chapter Ten. Here I discuss the cross-functional team as a learning community, team training in group process skills, leader development, technical training, and cross-training.

In Chapter Eleven, I discuss team size and make the point that smaller is better. I examine the tendency for cross-functional teams to be larger than is necessary and the negative impact of oversized teams on team productivity and on the involvement, participation, and trust of team members. I discuss optimal team size and what to do if your team is just too large.

Chapter Twelve focuses on the internal dynamics of a cross-functional team. Here I describe both barriers and methods of addressing issues such as conflicts among team members, lack of trust and openness, conduct of team meetings, the right mix of people, involvement of suppliers and customers, colocation of team members, and effective use of communications technology.

In Chapter Thirteen, I focus on management's role in building an organization that supports and encourages cross-functional teamwork. Here I provide a specific prescription for leaders of organizations who want to know what they can do to make teamwork thrive in their organizations.

Finally, in Chapter Fourteen, I outline what to do after you read this book and are ready to initiate a change. For each of you, I suggest ways to get started.

The book ends with Tools for Developing Cross-Functional Teams, consisting of several supplements to the ideas presented here. First, the series of case studies of cross-functional teams allows you to test your insight into the issues faced by cross-functional teams. Next, you can use the Survey of Cross-Functional Teamwork to assess the strengths and weaknesses of your team. In the section Read Any Good Books Lately? I provide an annotated bibliography of books about various aspects of teamwork. And finally, just for fun, I include my Top Ten Ways to Ensure the Failure of Teams.

ACKNOWLEDGMENTS

I begin by acknowledging the person who encouraged and supported me throughout the writing of this book and just about everything of value in my life—my wife, Judy Parker. Actually, her exact words were, "Well, when are you going to start the new book?" and then, later, "Is it done yet?"

Two close friends and professional colleagues were especially helpful. My graduate school roommate, collaborator on many team projects, and old friend, Ira Asherman, sent copies of articles, called with new ideas, and commented on the manuscript. Dick Kropp, my former client at Wang Laboratories, coauthor with me of *50 Activities for Team Building* (1992), and close friend, provided comments on the manuscript, sound ideas, and a general belief in me.

Another friend and colleague, Jerry McAdams, contributed a sound critique and detailed suggestions for improving the usefulness of Chapter Nine. Cedric Crocker, my editor at Jossey-Bass, offered support and specific comments throughout the development process.

Lawrenceville, New Jersey   Glenn M. Parker
February 1994

THE AUTHOR

Glenn M. Parker is an author and consultant who works with organizations to improve quality and productivity by creating high-performing teams. His best-selling book *Team Players and Teamwork: The New Competitive Business Strategy* (1990) was selected as one of the ten best business books of 1990 by Tom Brown, business book reviewer for National Public Radio and columnist for *Industry Week*. His training and team-building instruments, the *Parker Team Player Survey* (1991) and the *Team Development Survey* (1992), are fast becoming standards in the field. Glenn is also coauthor of *50 Activities for Team Building* (1992), which was selected by *Human Resource Executive* magazine as one of 1992's top ten training tools. His article on building a team-based organization, "Getting into Shape," was selected for inclusion in *Service Excellence: The Best of Managing Service Quality*, Vol. 2, edited by Rory Chase (1993). Parker is also a regular contributor to TODAY'S

TEAM, a monthly newsletter for team members, leaders, and facilitators.

Using his materials and instruments, Parker conducts team building with intact groups, as well as training workshops on team effectiveness. He works with start-up and ongoing teams of all types. His ideas, techniques, and advice have been used in many companies, including Merck and Company, Johnson & Johnson, Bristol-Myers Squibb, 3M, Asea Brown Bovari, the Budd Company, AT&T, NYNEX, Bell Communications Research, CIBA-GEIGY, Allied-Signal, Sun Microsystems, and the Environmental Protection Agency.

Parker holds a B.A. degree (1959) in economics from City College of New York and an M.A. degree (1961) in industrial relations from the University of Illinois and has done doctoral work in industrial relations at Cornell University. He is much in demand as a speaker and is a regular presenter at national conferences sponsored by the American Society for Training and Development (ASTD) and Lakewood Conferences. He is past president of the mid–New Jersey chapter of ASTD.

Parker lives in Lawrenceville, New Jersey, with his wife, Judy. In his spare time he plays tennis, roots for the Philadelphia 76ers, and plans his next vacation.

CROSS-
FUNCTIONAL
TEAMS

Why Cross-Functional Teams?

1

The Competitive Advantages of Cross-Functional Teams

The world and the world of business are changing. Individualism is out, teamwork is in. Specialization is out, a new-style generalism is in. Rigid organizational lines are out, fluid collaboration is in. Power is out, empowerment is in. Hierarchical organizations are out, replaced by network organizations, adaptive organizations, informal organizations, and horizontal organizations. Right smack in the middle of all this sit cross-functional teams composed of experts ready to move quickly and flexibly to adapt to changing business needs.

WORKING WITH
DIVERSE TEAM MEMBERS

Recent survey results (see Chapter Two), the large number of books (see References) and conferences, and plain old-fashioned observation tell us that teams have become an important business strategy in today's competitive environment. Central to this shift are a series of unusual collaborative efforts. These new-styled teams are composed of people from a variety of functions who may know and like each other, or who may be enemies, or who may simply be strangers.

Some Are Strangers

Sometimes team members have never met before the first team meeting. An automobile design engineer from Detroit may never have talked with a Ford dealer from Langhorne, Pennsylvania. The reason may not be simple geographical separation. A marketing professional may never have run into the government affairs attorney, even though they work in the same building.

Some Are Colleagues

Sometimes team members have worked together on past projects. For example, if the research scientist and the manufacturing manager have a common understanding of customer needs, their past association can help jump-start the team. However, if they are old turf-war enemies, the team will begin with a conflict to resolve.

Some Are Friends

Sometimes team members know each other but have never worked together. For instance, the social studies teacher and the English teacher have shared lunch and breaks together for years in the faculty room. Now, however, they are part of the seventh-grade team, which must develop a co-ordinated curriculum. The computer programmer and the accountant have carpooled together but now they must team up to develop a new tracking system. Sometimes informal associations play out well in more serious team environments, but not always.

THE CULTURE OF CROSS-FUNCTIONAL TEAMS

The diversity of cross-functional team players creates a new culture. Therefore, it is important to understand that in creating a cross-functional team, you are fashioning a potentially powerful organizational vehicle. While it lacks the simplicity of a functional team composed of, for example, six engineers all reporting to the engineering manager, a cross-functional team has a greater chance of realizing the potential of that old axiom, The whole is greater than the sum of its parts. This group of allies, enemies, and strangers can weave together a cross-functional design that is an amalgam of many cultures.

Team sponsors and team players must understand that the beauty of the idea of putting together a diverse group of people to launch a product, develop a new system, or solve a business problem is not enough. A good concept is not enough. Diversity is not enough. In practice, it requires the migration from a parochial view of the world—my function, my values, and my goals are paramount—to a broader view, that says, We're all in this together. Success is team success, rewards are team rewards, and if the team fails, the members share the blame. For a manager responsible for team development or a leader of a cross-functional team, the implications are clear:

- Insist on a clear team goal and a plan to achieve it.

- Work hard to gain the commitment of team members and other stakeholders to the team's goal.

- Emphasize collaborative efforts and team rewards.

- Provide training on how to work with a diverse group of people.

- Create a set of policies and procedures that support a team-based environment.

WORKING WITH STRANGERS: WHAT WORKS AND WHY

Effective cross-functional teams have many advantages. While some of the pluses apply to other types of teams too, these advantages have a unique flavor when played out in the context of a cross-functional team. I have found that cross-functional teams bring six important competitive advantages to organizations that successfully implement and manage these teams.

1. *Speed*. Cross-functional teams reduce the time it takes to get things done, especially in the product development process.
2. *Complexity.* Cross-functional teams improve an organization's ability to solve complex problems.
3. *Customer focus*. Cross-functional teams focus the organization's resources on satisfying the customer's needs.
4. *Creativity.* By bringing together people with a variety of experiences and backgrounds, cross-functional teams increase the creative capacity of an organization.
5. *Organizational learning*. Members of cross-functional teams are more easily able to develop new technical and professional skills, learn more about other disciplines, and learn how to work with people who have different team-player styles and cultural backgrounds than those who do not participate in cross-functional teams.
6. *Single point of contact*. The cross-functional team promotes more effective cross-team teamwork by identifying one place to go for information and for decisions about a project or customer.

SPEED

Speed—the capability to gets things done faster—is now so important for business success that time-based management is a topic of critical importance to businesses in competitive markets. Speed is a critical differentiating factor in product and systems development and in customer service.

In product development, cross-functional teams are central to reducing the time spent in the development cycle, or what is now called *time to market* or *time to value*. According to a McKinsey and Company study, the cost of arriving late to market by five months reduces gross profits by 25 percent (Wallace and Halverson, 1992). Cross-functional teams replace serial development with parallel development. In the past, the process was like a relay race, with completed work serving as the baton. When the people in a function completed their work (basic research, prototyping, testing, engineering, operations, marketing), they handed it off to the next group of people, who did their work and passed it on to strangers or colleagues in the next group, who did their work and passed it on to the next group.

Cross-functional teams allow many pieces of the development process to be done at the same time. The team approach also eliminates many of the features of the serial process that added time and costs to the final product. Operating in isolation, a department might add features that would seem valuable to them but not to others, including the customer. For example, engineers might give a product features that would make it difficult either to manufacture or sell. On the other hand, sales people might like to see features that make the product easier to sell but would add excessive production costs. All this isolated development activity can slow down the time to market because it leads to errors and other factors that require time-consuming changes down the line. Cross-functional teams discover these problems at the front end or simply catch them before they occur.

Honeywell's Building Controls Division uses cross-functional teams to cut product development time by at least 50 percent through minimizing changes in specifications and therefore in the subsequent rework. As the following description of Honeywell's process also makes clear, these are the very same capabilities critical for a successful total quality effort.

The reduction in changes and rework is achieved in part through an emphasis on the front end of the product development process. Through disciplined planning, team members produce a "frozen spec" that, once agreed to by the team, can only be changed by a "no-go" decision based on a major shift in the market's requirements. The team itself enforces the discipline necessary to defer small design changes to the second issue of the product under development. In addition to shortening the product development cycle, the process of arriving at a stable product design also benefits product manufacturability, cost, and quality. Getting production involved in the product development process from the start focuses the development team on designs that are compatible with existing manufacturing processes. It also enables the team to identify any hurdles in the early stages that will affect product cost, performance, or delivery [Larson, 1988, p. 23].

In all, the cross-functional teams at Honeywell's Building Controls Division are credited with

- cutting product development time by at least 50 percent
- reducing product costs by 5 to 10 percent
- producing products that are 97.6 percent defect-free
- enhancing the performance of new products in the market
- delivering products that meet customer requirements

Systems developers are finding that cross-organizational teams that bring users together with information systems professionals cut time and cost from the development of new systems. Team techniques such as IBM's Joint Application Design (JAD), WISE Integrated Systems Development Method (WISDM) from the Western Institute of Systems Engineering, and the Method developed by Performance Resources are group design methodologies that facilitate user-developer team dynamics. Cigna Insurance in Philadelphia,

CNA Insurance in Chicago, Chase Manhattan Bank, and Ford Motor Company in Dearborn, Michigan, are all committed to team techniques in systems design. Studies indicate that the development cycle can be cut in half with effective teamwork, resulting in an overall return on investment of 10 to 15 percent (Leavitt, 1987).

In 1988, Motorola was one of the first winners of the Malcolm Baldrige National Quality Award, because the company demonstrated it could successfully transform an old-line giant into a world-class, team-based, quality corporation. A study of its Austin, Texas, manufacturing plant revealed that cross-functional teams could successfully complete a number of important business projects (Kumar and Gupta, 1991). For example, when teams took over the experiments for process optimization, the results were completed in less time, and overall yields improved by 5 percent when compared with experiments done alone by the process engineer. Teams have also improved cycle time on a pilot line where new products are developed or new products are brought in from other sites. Cross-functional teams have also completed the installation of new equipment and the layout of a manufacturing area in record time.

One of the most dramatic stories concerns Cincinnati Milacron, an old-line machinery manufacturer. The company used a new cross-functional team process to develop a plastic injection molding machine in record time, at reduced cost and with increased functionality (Nulty, 1990). Instead of the engineering department designing a machine in their cubbyhole and then tossing it over the wall to manufacturing, purchasing, marketing, and others, a team composed of people from all the relevant departments was formed. They began with clear goals: to make the machine competitive with foreign imports by reducing costs by 40 percent, to increase functionality, and to cut the usual development cycle from two years to one. In the end, they cut the cycle time to 270 days (the project became known as the P-270) and met other cost and quality goals. And more important, the new machine is selling. In the first full year of production, the company has sold two-and-a-half times as many of the new machines as it had in the best year of the earlier model.

A notable example of the success of cross-functional teamwork is AT&T's development of the new 4200 cordless telephone (Dumaine, 1989). Vice President of Product Development John Hanley decided that the old development process, which took two years, was just not acceptable. Getting to the market faster was simply good business because the company can charge a premium while everyone else plays catch-up. Hanley replaced the traditional hand-off approach with small teams of engineers, manufacturers, and marketers who had the authority to make decisions on functionality, cost, production, and appearance. The teams set strict deadlines for freezing all design specs and held to them. As a result, they cut the development time from two years to twelve months while improving quality and, of course, lowering costs. Thus, there is no need to form a new team, obtain other resources, or re-negotiate the time line for providing the product or service to the customer. All customer needs can be met by the cross-functional team.

Speed Summarized

The examples just discussed provide some clues as to how cross-functional teams speed up the development process. Successful teams

- Have a clear goal
- Include all the relevant functions
- Involve all the key players from the very beginning of the process
- Enforce the discipline necessary to keep to a schedule

While teams are a key to improving an organization's time to market, it should be understood that other things must be in place if an organization is really going to effectively implement the concept of speed. Other factors include simplifying the approval process and the other red tape that slows down development, using the latest software tools to support development, and — here's a big one — top-management support for the team's goal.

COMPLEXITY

Cross-functional teams are in a better position than a series of functional teams to solve complex business problems, since most of these problems transcend disciplines or functions. The old view that you can put a genius alone in a laboratory or in front of a computer terminal, water and feed him or her periodically, and then wait for a solution to emerge is losing ground. As a manager in a telecommunications research and development company told me, "Network architecture planning is so broad a field that no one person can do it alone." The cross-functional team provides the framework for putting together scientists and engineers with a variety of backgrounds and diverse training to solve a complex business problem, design a new system, develop a new product, or reorganize the company. As the authors of a recent study of new-product teams said, "As products become more complex, it is no longer possible for a single engineer or scientist to complete a project alone" (Ancona and Caldwell, 1990b, p. 25). In our survey of cross-functional teamwork, creativity came up often as an outcome of cross-functional product development teams. Bringing people together from different parts of the company with different skill sets, a wide variety of orientations, and training in diverse disciplines means that the product outcomes will be more creative. It is not just reduced cycle time but as Barbara Bennett, vice president of The Stanley Works, put it in responding to my survey: "More innovative products result from cross-functional product development teams."

In a functional organization, many groups might be given the same problem to solve and then go off and work at it in isolation from each other. When the various solutions and recommendations come back, one person, or a task force, would sift through them and try to come up with a synthesis or simply pick one of the ideas. In this model, it is assumed that each group has enough information and background to look at the whole problem. This model offers no possibility of group interaction, cross-learning, or synergy.

Under the old system at Ford Motor Company, there was no collaboration between people who designed the exterior of the car and those who designed the interior. However, Mimi Vandermolen, an executive with Ford, saw the need for looking at the total design of the Probe as the problem to be solved. The problem was how to design an automobile that had appeal for both young men and women. As a result, she created an overall design team that began with a common vision of the target market for the car. Together, this cross-functional team of people who design the hood, fenders, and doors worked together with those who design the seats, steering wheel, and rearview mirror. Vandermolen reported that a cross-functional team of interior and exterior car designers "would allow us to avoid making mistakes in exterior design that would ultimately cause problems in interior design. For example, if the shape of the roof is already set in stone when you get ready to do the interior, you may have to sacrifice passenger space. But if you plan the interior and exterior together, you can create harmony between the two" ("Shifting the Corporate Culture," 1992, pp. 25, 28). In the end, this new team approach would save the company 20 percent on the cost of the design *and* produce a better vehicle.

In some cases, cross-functional teams in manufacturing are responsible for end-to-end product development. For example, at TRW in Cleveland, Ohio, Ian Ziskin, director of leadership and organizational effectiveness, reports that a transportation electronics team included people from engineering, manufacturing, quality, operations, finance, marketing, and even suppliers, such as Sony. The team was charged with the development of a remote, keyless entry for the automobile industry. They took responsibility for the product's design and manufacturing and, ultimately, taking it to market (interview with the author, January 1993).

Complexity Summarized

Keys to using cross-functional teams to solve complex business problems include

- A leader with a creative vision
- Freedom from unnecessary restrictions, including the freedom to fail
- A wide range of diverse opinion
- An openness on the part of team members to new ideas

CUSTOMER FOCUS

Every type of team — product development, systems development, sales, quality, or any other cross-functional team — has a customer (often these customers are internal to the organization). Therefore, by definition, all teams should have a customer focus.

As organizations around the world jump on the quality bandwagon, we are seeing a resurgence of teamwork as a serious business strategy. Every serious quality effort is a team-based effort. Every winner of the Malcolm Baldrige National Quality Award has made teams an integral part of the quality process. In fact, effective teamwork is one of the Baldrige criteria. And in quality improvement, cross-functional teams are seen as an important tool, especially when the product or service spans several functions.

As the work process becomes more complex, and as quality is defined as "satisfying the customer," cross-functional teams become a necessity for achieving quality improvements. For many products and services, one person or one department simply cannot know enough to understand the total process, identify the breakdown points, and suggest ways to reduce errors, waste, or other drains on quality. For example, the beginning of most quality improvement efforts is the creation of a process flowchart. In working this process with one of my clients, it became clear that producing the flowchart required the combined input of at least six different people, each with a unique view of the work process. In another case, we found that the production of a customer invoice involved several functions within a department as well as two other groups in other departments.

There are many examples of small and large companies, government agencies, and school systems using cross-functional teams to improve the quality of their products and services. Teams are part of corporatewide quality programs in major corporations, as well as in small, homegrown quality improvement efforts, school reform projects, and government agencies seeking ways to better serve their clients. Since we all know how Motorola, Xerox, IBM, Federal Express, and other high-profile companies are using teams to drive their successful quality efforts, let's look at some not so famous but effective organizations.

Storage Technology Corporation, a worldwide producer of storage and retrieval systems for the computer industry headquartered in Louisville, Colorado, used a team-based quality process that helped achieve an impressive business comeback (Stratton, 1991). The company went from the depths of Chapter 11 in 1984 to revenues in excess of one billion dollars in 1991, buttressed by significant increases in customer satisfaction ratings and revenue per employee.

Donald Stratton, StorageTek's vice president of corporate quality and education, reports that cross-functional teams, supported by an extensive training program, have been critical to quality improvements and the company's turnaround (interview with the author, January 1993). For example, a cross-functional metrology team, winner of the 1992 Chairman's Quality Award, made recommendations that led to reduced inventory of test sets (350 to fifty) and decreased interval of testing (twenty-eight days to three days). This saved StorageTek $500,000.

Some people may think that the old stodgy bureaucracy of a government agency would not be amenable to the team-based quality process, much less the idea of people working with others outside their immediate work area. These cynics only see resistance to change in government agencies, compounded by a view that says, "What's the point of process improvements? If we show we can do more with less, they'll just cut our budget next year." But the cynics would be wrong. I see many government agencies at all levels using cross-functional teamwork to improve services to the public.

Although many people would not point to the U.S. Department of Veterans Affairs as a paragon of innovation and change, they would miss an important example of successful teamwork. At the Philadelphia Regional Office and Insurance Center (ROIC), more than forty cross-functional quality teams have formed. The initial results of some of the teams have been impressive.

> One of the first teams tackled problems within the Veterans Insurance Phone Service, where each day telephone operators handle between 2,600 and 3,000 calls from veterans and their beneficiaries. In the 21 months that the eight-person team met, it reduced the percentage of multiple calls reps receive (when a customer calls more than once to get the same information) from a high of 12.9 percent in January 1990 to a low of 3.3 percent the following August. . . . Another team saved the department an estimated $168,000 by simplifying the office's loan-default processes (veterans can borrow mortgage funds from the ROIC) [Penzer, 1991, p. 36].

The interesting aspect of this team-based quality program is that while cost savings are a natural outcome of teamwork, other factors may prove more important in the long term. Less tangible but potentially more powerful is the learning that comes from understanding the total work process, including all the tasks and how they fit together. Serving on a cross-functional team has helped employees understand how a screw-up in their area impacts work in other areas. In addition, individual employees get a sense of ownership and empowerment from participating on a team that generates ideas that eventually see the light of day.

One radical innovation using cross-functional teams is taking place in the Kentucky school system. The power to make key decisions about textbooks, courses, and teacher selection has been taken from local school boards and handed over to school-based councils comprised of the principal, three teachers, and two parents. In this case, the customers are parents and students. While each of Kentucky's 1,366 schools has considerable control over the education of their children, they are also accountable for results. Each school is also rewarded if test scores, attendance records, graduation rates, and other standards increase significantly. The rewards involve monetary payments, which can be used to supplement teachers' salaries or make school improvements. The reward system is also designed to encourage teamwork in the school among teachers and other professionals because the awards are given to the schools rather than to individuals. In other words, if the school does well, the staff does well. Therefore, they are more likely to share ideas and resources with their colleagues. On the other hand, schools that do poorly will be declared "in crisis," which will trigger the dispatching of a team of experts to devise a rescue plan.

Here in one place we find some important factors for achieving success in cross-functional teamwork. The factors are a small group of key players, given sufficient authority to make important decisions; measures of success provided in advance; and rewards for success given to the entire team (Henkoff, 1991b; Dowler, 1991).

In a local school district in New Jersey, junior high school teachers in a variety of disciplines are teaming up to provide quality education. For example, an eighth-grade-level team includes five teachers — English, social studies, math, science, and foreign language — and specialists at various times in areas such as physical education, industrial arts, the library, art, and music. The team meets regularly to correlate the learning between subjects.

- When the English class is reading a novel set during the American Revolution, the social studies teacher will devote several lessons to the historical background.

- The art teacher presents a unit on lettering at the same time the English teacher leads a unit entitled Designs in Art and Poetry.

- When the math teacher is teaching a unit on probability and statistics, the science teacher has a lesson on analyzing data.

The team coordinates field trips and midterm examinations. When one teacher takes the class to a museum, the other teachers do lessons related to the museum topic. The team can also schedule tests so they do not all fall on the same day. In addition, teachers can discuss and develop a coordinated game plan for students with behavior problems. Thus far, teachers in the program report that students are more motivated and there appear to be fewer discipline problems. The students realize they are part of a team and seem to enjoy the competitive spirit that is associated with the team concept. In the future, the cross-functional team concept in a school should result in some positive shifts in the total organization. For example, assistant principals would be able to spend more time on real administrative and planning work and less on discipline. Perhaps there would be fewer curriculum coordinators and department heads, or their role would change to focus more on strategic planning, coaching, and staff development.

In many ways, the advent of teamwork in the sales area amounts to the most radical application of the cross-functional team model. Think about it. Teamwork among salespeople is the last bastion of rugged individualism and entrepreneurship in most organizations. And yet, even here, and especially here, organizations are finding a real payoff from cross-functional teamwork.

One reason cross-functional selling teams are emerging is that customers are demanding them. People in client companies are saying, "We're tired of dealing with a cadre of salespeople from your company. Most of your people do not even know each other, and as a result, there is no coordination among the product lines." In an often-repeated story, two sales representatives from the same company meet each other at the elevator in a client's office and begin trading stories about the client. At that moment, the client comes by and proceeds to introduce them to each other. Only then do these two strangers realize that they work for the same company.

In the health care industry, there is a trend away from the traditional fee-for-service to managed health care. Managed care includes providers such as health maintenance organizations (HMOs) and large hospital systems as well as payors such as Blue Cross/Blue Shield and commercial insurance companies. As a result, pharmaceutical companies are focusing their sales efforts on large providers, such as HMOs (Cigna, US Healthcare) and hospital systems (Humana, the Veterans Health Administration). The objective is to build multiyear, multiproduct, bundled accounts that increase profitability. There are indications that this strategy is working. In some cases, by providing competitive pricing, quality products, and excellent service, a drug company has been able to get an HMO to use a particular product to the exclusion of a competitor's drug. At the same time, these emerging large customers are demanding a coordinated approach from the drug companies. They want the advantages of dealing with a supplier that offers lower prices, a knowledge of their business, a single point of contact, and a day-to-day responsiveness to their needs. In this new environment, an account management or team-selling approach makes sense for everyone.

This approach requires the identification of a small number of large accounts for which a team strategy is appropriate. This step is usually simple, with companies applying a variation of the old 80–20 rule — 80 percent of our business comes from 20 percent of our customers. The goal then becomes one of developing a business plan for each customer by bringing together the key marketers from each product line. While everyone agrees that a coordinated approach is logical, the trick is to get agreement on a plan and give the team sufficient authority to act. One barrier is that a plan may result in increased revenues for the total company created by increased sales for one product line but decreased sales for another. The team has to keep its eye on the overall goal of increasing company revenues. Companies that take the long view of building a relationship with a customer rather than just trying to make a sale are able to make this team-selling approach work.

One of the innovators in this area is Procter & Gamble, which years ago acted to reduce the number of salespeople calling on retailers (Sellers, 1992). In addition, people from marketing, finance, distribution, and operations work with sales to coordinate efforts with large customers. These sales teams help big accounts such as Eckerd Drugs and Kroger solve practical business problems, which ultimately helps these large retailers sell more Procter & Gamble products.

Another large company using a team approach to oversee sales to large accounts is Black and Decker. In one successful strategy, the company "set up Wal-Mart and Home Depot divisions to cater specifically to those fast-growing accounts. In each, a vice president oversees a group composed of salespeople, marketer, an information systems expert, a sales forecaster, and a financial analyst. The team can be rallied to create a promotion, such as a specially designed package containing a drill and drill bits for the retailer. The result: Black and Decker sales to Wal-Mart were up over 10% last year, and those to Home Depot climbed almost 40%" (Sellers, 1992, p. 102).

Cross-functional team selling does not work just for major corporations. Small businesses can bring together all the key players to increase sales and customer service. The mortgage banking industry is one such example. The number of mortgage bankers has increased dramatically as a number of independent mortgage companies have sprung up. These companies aggressively sell mortgages to the home buyers and owners who are refinancing and then resell the "paper" to major lending institutions. As a recent refinancing customer of a local mortgage company, I can attest to the cross-functional teamwork required to close a deal. The team includes the sales representative, loan processor, underwriter, file clerk, receptionist, and other back office people never seen by the customer. Ancillary, but no less important, team members include the mortgage insurer, appraiser, and attorney. In the case of a home purchase, the realtor is also a key member of the sales team.

In a totally different market, BSD, a software inventory control company, uses cross-functional teams that are responsible for selling, designing, installing, and servicing specific customers in a particular area (Belasco, 1991). BSD is the most profitable business of its kind, with sales in excess of $500 million, built on the strength of seven hundred people organized into sixty-two teams around the world, according to James Belasco, a San Diego–based consultant to the company (interview with the author, January 1993). Each team is responsible for hiring, training, and maintaining sales and service to customers in their area. Their success is built on cross-training of all team members and a reward system tied to team success.

Cross-functional team selling lends itself to high-tech industries where product sales and after-sales support require a high level of technical expertise. The computer industry is a good example, because sales requires working with the buyer to get the right mix of hardware, software, and support. Cathy Hyatt Hills, a sales-training consultant from Novato, California, says that sales teams include sales representatives, engineers, programmers, and, perhaps, lawyers, accountants, financing experts, and others (interview with the author, January 1993).

According to Hills, Pacific Bell is one company that has encouraged vendors to not only use cross-functional sales teams but to integrate them into their internal project teams. This cross-functional and cross-organizational team approach has "prevented costly mistakes...and improved the company's bottom line by getting new technology up and running more quickly than otherwise would have been possible" (Hills, 1992, p. 56).

Customer Focus Summarized

Using cross-functional teams to put the customer first requires

- A clear understanding of who is the team's customer
- Involving the customer closely, either directly as a team member or indirectly with consistent communication
- Training for team members in process-improvement techniques and team dynamics
- Empowerment of the team to make decisions that satisfy customer needs
- Rewards that support and encourage collaboration

CREATIVITY

Cross-functional teams provide the basis for a creative mix of people with different backgrounds, orientations, cultural values, and styles. While this diversity can be hell to manage, the possibilities for bright new ideas and innovations to bubble up are great. In some organizations, these teams spring up like wildflowers; people with an idea or a problem simply call other people and say, "Let's get together and talk about making this part withstand heat better," or "How about a brainstorming session on making it easier for the customer to get this service on the weekend?" Some organizations foster this type of ad hoc collaboration by providing such simple things as flip charts or white boards in the hallways as well as more substantive support, such as time and budget, to pursue an idea.

In every organization, an informal organization exists

side-by-side with the formal bureaucracy. Sometimes called the emergent organization or adaptive organization, it is the latter-day version of what, more than twenty years ago, Warren Bennis labeled "the temporary society" (Bennis and Slater, 1968). Cross-functional teams embody the positive features of the informal organization because they provide the opportunity for creative expression usually preserved for small entrepreneurial companies. The team achieves this by being a venue for aligning what the organization seeks — innovation — with what excites creative people — an opportunity to use their heads and learn from each other (Dumaine, 1991).

Companies in computers, telecommunications, and automobiles are especially supportive of cross-functional teams because of those industries' rapidly changing markets and the need for constant innovation. Other companies, such as Rubbermaid and 3M, which bet their future on product innovations, use cross-functional teams to drive the process. Both companies have a goal that says 30 percent of their sales will come from products introduced in the last five years.

As Motorola has shown, cross-functional teams at all levels in the organization have been a vehicle for creative problem solving: "the Ronamakers [are] a group of workers around the world who manage inventory for Motorola's automotive and industrial group, which stocks things such as microprocessors and transistors. These employees, mostly high school graduates, started using basic industrial engineering techniques to analyze inventory and ultimately reduce average levels of supply to four weeks from nearly seven, saving $2.4 million a year" (Hill and Yamada, 1992, p. A18).

Creativity can be found in all parts of the organization when teams of colleagues and strangers from different parts of the company come together with the freedom to look at new ways of doing business. At Southwest Industries, a high-technology aerospace engineering company, cross-functional shift teams have produced some dramatic breakthroughs in quality improvement. Composed of machine operators, electricians, maintenance mechanics, and tool and dye makers, the teams were given responsibilities for quality previously handled by quality control inspectors: "Under the previous system, by the time quality control inspectors found a problem, 25 to 30 more airplane frames had been run before the operation could be closed down and the cause found and corrected. Now the team members usually find the problem early on and correct it. Work in progress inventory is down, output per shift is up, and the two inspectors are no longer needed" (Robinson, Oswald, Swinehart, and Thomas, 1991, p. 14).

Creativity Summarized

Cross-functional teams can be a vehicle for fostering creativity if

- The culture supports informal problem solving
- Risk taking is encouraged and rewarded
- Product and service innovations are seen as critical to the organization's future

ORGANIZATIONAL LEARNING

The value of the cross-functional team as a "learning community" is rarely proposed. Since the emphasis is on the ever-present bottom line, "soft" benefits such as education and training are not given sufficient emphasis. However, it is all those things above the line that makes for a profitable bottom line.

In many cases, employee learning in cross-functional teams is informal; it happens as a natural result of opportunities to interact with colleagues and strangers who have knowledge and skills to share. At team meetings, presentations of proposals and status reports on topics related to the team's goals are a development source. In addition, opportunities to ask questions and participate in discussions take place throughout the life of the team. Teams also have subcommittees, which offer another way to learn from colleagues.

Even less formal is the networking that is part of the team process. People tell me that the cross-functional team is a place to learn from colleagues and strangers during those periods prior to meetings, during breaks, after the meetings, or over lunch. These contacts become resources for development in other settings and on other topics. An engineer at a telecommunications company told me she learned more about the business through interactions with associates at project team meetings than from any other source.

Formal training is, of course, a major benefit of cross-functional teams. Since many of these teams are part of the quality improvement process, the members usually receive training in a variety of problem-solving techniques. Although the training is the usual fare, it pops up in some unusual places. For example, the Philadelphia office of the Department of Veterans Affairs (referred to earlier in this chapter) set up some forty cross-functional quality teams to improve the focus on the customer. The training included "learning about the customer-centered culture, statistical process control, group dynamics and error prevention" (Penzer, 1991, p. 34). While the advantages to the organization on one level were apparent—costs were reduced, customers were satisfied—on another level, they created a multiskilled work force. A knowledge of group dynamics and problem-solving tools will be helpful to the company in the future, when employees team up with people from other functions.

I recall one of my clients saying that while he valued the teamwork skills that his people were acquiring as they dealt with solving the current business problem, he was really interested in building a team-based culture over the long term. Over time, his organization did just that: it had a recognition program; the visible support of the managers; inclusion of team behaviors in performance appraisal; and a management team that served as a model of teamwork. In subsequent chapters, I will discuss each of these areas and provide examples of organization supports for cross-functional teams.

Cross-functional teams are often involved in what I will call formal technical training. There are two types of technical training: (1) The entire team learns the tools and techniques necessary for completing the work of the team, and (2) individual team members acquire the skills and knowledge of other jobs on the team. An offshoot of individual training is cross-training, where individual team members train each other in their specific skills and job knowledge.

Team Learning

The work of many teams requires the use of tools and technology. For example, many engineering project teams, utilizing a concept called concurrent engineering, need to learn how to use new hardware and software tools to support the design and development process. Litton Guidance and Control Systems in Woodland Hills, California, purchased Valid Logic Systems software and Sun Microsystems workstations. The company then provided classroom training on how to use the new tools, and an applications person from Valid came on-site every two weeks to answer questions. After some field experience, the classroom sessions were repeated in order to give the engineers an opportunity to ask questions and reinforce the learning based on actual use of the system (Beckert, 1991).

Team learning may also involve sessions conducted at team meetings covering basic information about the technical aspects of the team's project. Members of the team with the expertise conduct subject-matter training and orientation classes for other team members.

Individual Learning

In many cross-functional teams in manufacturing, cross-training is the key to a successful team. In this model, each team member acquires the skills of other team members' jobs and is therefore able to back up team members, detect errors in work, and participate more effectively in problem solving on intricate technical issues. Sometimes this training is done by other team members; other times it is conducted by supervisors and plant trainers. Companies such as Johnson and Johnson and Motorola have knowledge-based (also called skill-based) pay systems that provide pay increments for team members who successfully complete training programs and can demonstrate the new skill or knowledge. (More on this subject in Chapter Nine.)

Many organizations offer workshops in team communications that focus on learning to understand, appreciate, and communicate with a variety of team members, who have a variety of team-player styles. It is also important to include knowledge of different cultures and what people from these cultures bring to the team. We know that teams which are both cross-functional and cross-cultural provide rich opportunities to learn how to work with a diverse group of people (Halverson, 1992). In Chapter Ten I outline a variety of training and development activities for cross-functional teams.

Team Learning Summarized

To take advantage of the learning opportunities provided by cross-functional teams, it helps to

- Provide training that breaks down the barriers between strangers
- Conduct technical training that demystifies the work of the various functions on the team
- Create an open environment, which allows informal learning to flourish
- Reward team members who share information and expertise and team members who are active learners

SINGLE POINT OF CONTACT

In the functional team structure, it is often difficult to figure out where to go for information when working on a complex, long-term project. Because development in this structure is done serially, it is often hard to get an accurate and complete overview of the status, resources, and impact of the project. A major drawback of this approach is the lack of a shared vision. Functional team participants are usually more concerned about getting their piece of the puzzle complete than they are about seeing that the total project gets done. When a conflict arises between the project and their own department, you can be sure who wins.

In addition to the lack of a shared vision and commitment to the project, there is no good mechanism to coordinate the varied efforts. Some years ago, organizations using a matrix management structure resorted to the creation of "integrators," whose job it was to facilitate the coordination of the various allies, enemies, and strangers assigned to a project. The cross-functional team structure and process plays this role now: "a [cross-functional] team becomes the single point of contact for all corporate functions involved in day-to-day development work and for managers within each function. The manufacturing team member, for example, serves as the core team's liaison with the manufacturing vice president and the manufacturing engineers assigned to the project. . . . The team system shifts employee focus away from specific divisions, departments, or other functional groups to the project itself, as the team members become accountable for achieving the project's goals" (Whiting, 1991, p. 50).

The automobile industry uses the cross-functional team as the single point of contact for the complex job of bringing a vehicle to market. Chrysler coined the term *platform teams* to describe cross-functional groups charged with "bringing a vehicle to market — on time, within budget, and with world class quality characteristics" (Vasilash, 1992, p. 59). Platform teams include engineers, manufacturing experts, marketing professionals, and suppliers, among others. And the teams are effective. They have reduced time to market by twelve months and improved quality. One way they did this was to run pilot production vehicles earlier in the cycle. A team developed the LH midsize sedans (Chrysler Concorde, Dodge Intrepid,

Eagle Vision) as a platform, discovering 93 percent of all problems by week 35 and resolving 55 percent of all problems by then as well. Does this new use of cross-functional teams make a difference? Industry watchers seem to think so. In its year-end round-up of 1992's new product innovations, *Fortune* (December 28) highlighted the Chrysler LH Series for its "groundbreaking design" and surprisingly moderate price. Platform teams are given credit for the success of the LH series, which was named car of the year (1992) by *Automobile Magazine*.

Amoco Production Company provides us with another unusual example of cross-functional teamwork (Henkoff, 1991a). Several years ago, in an era of higher production costs and cheaper oil, the company decided that it needed to lower overhead and improve its operating effectiveness. A corner-stone of the strategy was the creation of cross-functional teams invested with authority to make decisions and charged with being the focal point for coordinating the various change efforts.

In one example, the Offshore Business Unit in New Orleans formed a cross-functional team made up of geologists, geophysicists, engineers, and computer scientists. The team was responsible for obtaining more oil from fields in the Gulf of Mexico. Using powerful new workstations and no longer reliant on the company's mainframe computer, the team worked together to find more oil in an area that had already been explored. In the old functional organization, each of these specialists would have been off in his or her own little world, linked to a vertical chain of command. Now, with the authority to act, the necessary technological support, and effective teamwork, this team continues to show results. For example, "Last year (1990) the offshore unit replaced more than 100 percent of its depleted reserves, an exceptionally good record in a mature province" (Henkoff, 1991a, p. 84).

In the sales arena, account teams (discussed earlier) serve as the single point of contact for all communication with the key company players and the client. In fact, it's inaccurate to call these major account teams "sales teams" because they include many other functions besides sales and do many other things in addition to selling.

One of my clients uses cross-functional teams to do a wide variety of things, from developing a new system to creating a vision for the future of the organization to planning the annual division conference. Anyone in the organization who has an idea, comment, or criticism knows where to go and can be sure it will get consideration. Team members also serve as a communication link with their groups, keeping them informed about the progress of the team's work and soliciting their ideas on the team's project.

The U.S. Environmental Protection Agency (EPA) has begun a fascinating experiment in cross-functional teamwork aimed at, among other things, creating one clear agency voice to speak to its "customers" (industry and environmental groups). These EPA "cluster teams" bring together people from many different offices to create a total approach to specific environmental issues (Cleland-Hamnett and Retzer, 1993). The regulated community (EPA's customers) benefits from this collaborative effort because it eliminates duplication of efforts by various agency offices, reduces compliance costs and hassles, sends a consistent EPA message to the community, and results in more innovative alternatives to environmental problems. While the cultural and structural barriers in the agency are significant, the EPA is moving forward with more than a dozen cluster teams, because they have seen some tangible benefits from a single point of contact. For example, the Pulp and Paper Industry Cluster decided to develop two key air and water regulations together, which will result in "an optimal combination of technologies to meet air and water requirements, avoid unnecessary cross-media pollution transfers,... minimize releases to air and water... and reduce compliance costs to the industry" (Cleland-Hamnett and Retzer, 1993, pp. 19–20). I have had a chance to work with the EPA cluster program and I see it as a model for cross-functional teamwork throughout government.

LEARNING FROM EXPERIENCE

Much can be learned from the experiences of organizations that have experimented with cross-functional teams. From these reports of successful teams, the keys to successful cross-functional teamwork appear to be as follows:

1. Management support in the form of tangible resources, encouragement of risk taking, and empowerment is critical.

2. A clear overarching goal that transcends individual functional priorities and commands the commitment of team members is essential.

3. Team awards must correspond to and support collaborative efforts.

4. The organization should provide training to help colleagues and strangers work together effectively and should encourage an open learning environment.

5. The team should include the right mix of players, including a leader able to pull together a diverse group of people in support of team goals.

6. The team should have the authority to act consistent with its responsibilities.

2

The Strategy
of Teams

In his fascinating personal account of life inside a Wall Street brokerage house, Michael Lewis describes the lack of cross-functional collaboration: "The salesmen blamed the traders, and the traders blamed the salesman. Why couldn't we sell their bonds to stupid European investors? the traders wanted to know. Why couldn't they find bonds that weren't so embarrassingly awful? the salesmen wanted to know. I was told by one trader, who was trying to off-load an AT&T style rip-off onto one of my customers, that I needed to be more of a team player. I was tempted to ask, 'What team?'" (Lewis, 1989, p. 195).

What team, indeed. Lewis's colleagues at Salomon Brothers just didn't get it. They did not see that the winning strategy was teamwork among people from different parts of the organization, all focused on serving the customer. It is clearly one of the reasons the company subsequently fell on hard times. Salomon just didn't get it. But other companies are getting it.

The eleventh annual *Training* magazine study of some 1,600 organizations on the state of training and development in the United States reports that 82 percent of companies in their study have teams. And in organizations that have teams, an average of 53 percent of the employees are team members (Gordon, 1992). By the way, 1992 was the first year that questions on teams were included in the *Training* report, signaling the coming of age of teams as a topic for inquiry. Increasingly, teams are focusing on a wide variety of business issues: quality improvement, customer service, account management, product development, systems development, problem solving, strategic planning, and project management. In other words, the new look of teamwork in organizations includes many complex variations on the standard business team of the past — the boss and his or her direct reports.

The composition of teams in organizations is also changing. For example, when I recently asked a group attending a human resources conference who was on their teams, the response went something like this: "Well, we have people from finance, manufacturing, operations, marketing, engineering, a key customer, and even our major suppliers." What's being described here is a typical product development team in a manufacturing company. Other people talk about sales teams that include several different sales representatives, technical experts, financial analysts, customer service personnel, and, often, buyers from the customer's organization. Still others will describe a continuous improvement team made up of people from operations, purchasing, engineering, design, quality, and a representative of the key supplier.

The number of these cross-functional teams is growing as organizations see the advantages of a multidisciplinary approach and learn how to make it effective. The 1992 *Training* magazine study reported that among employees who belong to some kind of team, 18 percent belong to a cross-functional team (Gordon, 1992). That number will increase. For example, "84 percent of U.S. health care organizations and 60 percent of

Canadian health care organizations currently report that fewer than 25 percent of their employees are involved in cross-functional teams. It is expected that, three years into the future, about 45 percent of these same organizations will have 26 to 74 percent of their employees involved in quality-related teams" (Anderson, 1992, p. 35). A recent Wilson Learning Corporation study of teamwork practices reported that all "participants anticipate an increase in the use of all types of teams in their organizations. However, the greatest antici-pated increase tends to be in the expanded use of cross-functional teams" (Leimbach, 1992, p. 4).

What are the advantages of these teams? The response to this question varies widely from such pluses as speeding up the process and preventing problems down the road to serving the customer better and pooling expertise from a variety of sources. The key is that people believe the concept of the cross-functional team makes sense for today's complex busi-ness world. The challenge is how to deal with the barriers to success. The timing is right to figure out how to make team-work work because we are riding a crest of positive feeling about the potential of teams. The recent *Training* magazine survey reports that people feel that teams have produced significant improvements in organizations (Gordon, 1992, p. 64):

> Seventy-six percent said teams have improved employee morale.
>
> Sixty-two percent felt teams improved management's morale.
>
> Eighty percent reported that teams have contributed to increased profits.
>
> Ninety percent agreed that teams have improved the quality of products or services.
>
> Eighty-five percent said that teams have improved the level of customer service.
>
> Eighty-one percent felt teams have improved productivity.

WHAT IS A TEAM?

There are many ways to categorize teams. One way is to look at them in terms of three dimensions—of purpose, duration, and membership.

Purpose

Teams vary in their purpose or goal; for example, they may be devoted to product development, systems development, quality improvement, problem solving, or reengineering.

Duration

Teams tend to be either permanent or temporary. Permanent teams include the functional department teams and others that are built into the ongoing organizational structure. In other words, you can find them on the company's organization chart. Temporary teams include task forces, problem-solving teams, project teams, and a variety of short-term teams set up to develop, analyze, or study a business issue.

Membership

The membership of a team can be either functional or cross-functional. The basic business team in a department tends to be functional, whereas nowadays product development teams are usually cross-functional.

TEAMS VERSUS GROUPS

Despite what we call them, not all "teams" are teams. Some so-called teams are really simply groups, masquerading as teams because in today's world it's important to be on something called a "team." Keep in mind that there is nothing wrong with being a part of an effective group. For example, nine group leaders report to a division head. Each group leader has a set of objectives for which he or she is accountable. However, there is no overarching goal for which all nine are mutually accountable; interdependence only exists among several subsets of the group leaders. There is no joint product or service for which the whole group is responsible. Therefore, this is a group, not a team. Nevertheless, this can be a very effective structure.

A team is a group of people with a high degree of interdependence, geared toward the achievement of a goal or the completion of a task. In other words, team members agree on a goal and agree that the only way to achieve the goal is to work together. There are many groups with common goals that are not teams. The key is the requirement for interdependence. The three best-known types of teams today are functional teams, self-directed teams, and cross-functional teams.

The Functional Team

The classic functional team is a boss and his or her direct reports. This so-called military model has been the staple of modern business. Despite all the talk about change, most organization charts still look like a pyramid. It may be a flatter pyramid but it is a pyramid nevertheless. There is comfort in having all the design engineers report to the same manager. Engineers like hanging out with other engineers and other people like knowing where they can easily find an engineer. Issues such as authority, relationships, decision making, leadership, and boundary management are simple and clear.

The Self-Directed Team

There are as many ways of describing a self-directed team as there are consulting firms specializing in the process. For example, Development Dimensions International says that "a self directed team is an intact group of employees who are responsible for a 'whole' work process or segment that delivers a product or service to an internal or external customer. To varying degrees, team members work together to improve their operations, handle day-to-day problems, and plan and control their work. In other words, they are responsible not only for getting their work done but also for managing themselves" (Wellins, Byham, and Wilson, 1991, p. 3).

Zenger-Miller emphasizes team size, cross-training, and individual team member responsibility, when it defines a self-directed team as

> a highly trained group of employees, from 6 to 18, on average, fully responsible for turning out a well-defined segment of finished work. The segment could be a final product, like a refrigerator or ball bearing; or a service like a fully processed insurance claim. It could also be a complete but intermediate product or service, like a finished refrigerator motor, an aircraft fuselage, or the circuit plans for a television set. Because every member of the team shares equal responsibility for this finished segment of work, self-directed teams represent the conceptual opposite of the assembly line, where each worker assumes responsibility for a narrow technical function [Orsburn, Moran, Musselwhite, and Zenger, 1990, p. 8).

From Pfeiffer and Company we get a narrower conception of a self-directed team. Consultants Torres and Spiegel seem to limit self-directed teams to a functional area in the production side of organizations. In their view, "A self-directed team is a functional group of employees (usually between eight and fifteen members) who share responsibility for a particular unit of production. The work team consists of trained individuals who possess the technical skills and abilities necessary to complete all assigned tasks. Management has delegated to the self-directed work team the authority to plan, implement, control, and improve all work processes" (Torres and Spiegel, 1990, p. 3). While it is true that self-directed teams are more prevalent in production operations, especially in manufacturing, they also operate in the service side of a business. For example, many insurance companies have established self-directed teams in policyholder services.

Self-directed teams have been particularly successful in start-up sites. In these locations there is no history or culture to change, no supervisors to retrain, and no power shift to negotiate. There are many advantages to self-directed teams but there are tremendous obstacles to successful implementation, especially in hierarchical organizations that have no tradition of participative management or employee involvement. Many organizations are experimenting with self-directed teams for the wrong reasons — the most attractive reason being that it looks like an easy way to reduce the middle management and supervisory ranks. On the other hand, there are a small number of quality companies that are sincerely dedicated to successful self-management, and they are making it work.

The Cross-Functional Team

Sometimes called multidisciplinary teams (in educational settings, interdisciplinary teams), cross-functional teams are part of the quiet revolution that is sweeping across organizations today. There seems to be no limit to the possibilities for cross-functional teams. I have found them in a wide variety of industries doing an equally wide spectrum of business functions that were once done in isolation. To begin, it is important to understand that "a standard cross-functional team is composed of those individuals from departments within the firm whose competencies are essential in achieving an optimal evaluation. Successful teams combine skill-sets which no single individual possesses" (Doyle, 1991, p. 20). Many cross-functional teams are involved in product development where "members of different departments and disciplines are brought together under one manager and given the charge to make development decisions and enlist support for them throughout the organization" (Ancona and Caldwell, 1992, p. 2). It is important to note that the role of the cross-functional team in using the expertise of many different people is coupled with the task of *enlisting support* for the work of the team. This is critical for successful cross-functional teamwork (I will discuss this further in Chapter Seven).

Team Composition. While some people question the viability of mixing people from different levels on the same team, at Motorola's assembly plant in Austin, Texas, this is not seen as a problem but rather as an advantage. People at Motorola believe that "members of a true cross-functional team should consist of all levels of management, operators, and technicians, and members from different organizations, including vendors and customers" (Kumar and Gupta, 1991, p. 32). In addition to including all levels, these Motorola teams also include "outsiders"—vendors and customers—making the teams both cross-functional and cross-organizational. Chapter Twelve discusses the value of involving suppliers and customers.

At 3M's Industrial Specialties Division, cross-functional teams literally manage the whole business. Each product family (for example, adhesives, fasteners, urethane films) is managed by a cross-functional team that includes people from the laboratory, manufacturing, and sales who are responsible for the daily operation of the business as well as new-product development (McKeown, 1990). Other companies, such as Pratt & Whitney and Hoffman La Roche, have reorganized parts of their businesses into product centers or specific lines of business with cross-functional teams driving the process. In some parts of the electronics industry, product development teams are called *core teams*, which are composed of eight to ten people from different functions involved in the day-to-day development of new products. They are "the single point of contact for all corporate functions involved in a development project, both for those involved in day-to-day development work and for managers within each function" (Whiting, 1991, p. 50).

Many consulting firms have reorganized their staffs into permanent multidisciplinary teams aligned with specific customers or market segment. ABB-Environmental Services, a subsidiary of Asea Brown Bovari based in Portland, Maine, recently eliminated all its functional departments in favor of ongoing customer-focused teams composed of geologists, hydrogeologists, environmental engineers, chemists, and other specialists. What's new about this approach is that the teams are part of the permanent structure of the organization.

Talk of permanent team structures causes some cynics

to suggest that cross-functional teams are simply a warmed-over version of the matrix organization popular in the 1960s (Davis and Lawrence, 1977). While some of the issues (such as the sharing of resources) are similar, no cross-functional team leaders I know or have studied see themselves as the typical two-boss manager found in matrix structures. Cross-functional teams are more akin to project organizations that must integrate various resource groups to achieve an agreed-upon product.

For the purposes of this book, I define a cross-functional team as: a group of people with a clear purpose representing a variety of functions or disciplines in the organization whose combined efforts are necessary for achieving the team's purpose. The team may be permanent or ad hoc and may include vendors and customers as appropriate.

WHICH TEAM?
WHEN AND WHERE?

Each type of team has its advantages and works best in a particular organizational setting.

1. *Functional teams* work well in traditional hierarchical organizations in stable, slow-growth industries with predictable markets.

2. *Self-directed teams* can be used in some of the same industries as functional teams and in many others as well, particularly in start-up sites or in organizations with an embedded base of participative management and a history of employee involvement.

3. *Cross-functional teams* seem to be most effective in companies with fast-changing markets, such as the computer, telecommunications, and similar industries that value adaptability, speed, and an intense focus on responding to customer needs.

So far, all of this looks pretty rosy. Just put together a group of people from different parts of the organization and let them go. Not so. Unspoken in all this discussion are the potential differences among the team players who come from different functions, different levels, and from outside the formal organization. Some players may be friendly colleagues with positive team experiences, some may be antagonists with memories of past wars, while still others may simply have never met. Cross-functional team members must see the team as more than a joining of functions; they must also see it as a blend of real people with different histories, team player styles, and priorities.

There are many obstacles to successful cross-functional teamwork. In the next chapter I outline the challenges and set the stage for the remainder of the book, which focuses on specific tools for creating effective cross-functional teams.

PART TWO

Effective Teamwork

C H A P T E R

3

Overcoming Barriers and Obstacles to Teamwork

Despite the obvious advantages of cross-functional teamwork, it is not as easy as it looks. There are many obstacles. Each obstacle is significant, can limit the effectiveness of cross-functional collaboration, and can even bring down a team. That's the bad news. The good news is that we know how to deal with each of these barriers. The remainder of this book is devoted to a detailed exploration of each of these issues and to a series of recommendations for overcoming the barriers. However, before we look at the barriers, let's put it all in a framework for understanding the dimensions of effective cross-functional teamwork.

43

THE THREE DIMENSIONS
OF EFFECTIVE TEAMWORK

Effective cross-functional teamwork includes an emphasis on three areas:

- Managing yourself—being an effective team player
- Managing the inside—being an effective team
- Managing the outside—building effective interteam relationships

Being an Effective Team Player

Teamwork starts with the individual—you and me—what I call the team player. A team is a collection of individuals, and therefore, what each of us brings to the party can make a difference in team success or failure. I believe that to the extent that each of us can be effective as a team player, to that extent the team can be effective. And equally important: To the extent that each person can increase his or her effectiveness, to that extent the team can increase its effectiveness. On a cross-functional team, each team member is there to contribute in a specific way to the goals of the team. When each team player lives up to his or her potential as a team participant, the team has an excellent chance of being successful. When one or more of the team players do not do what is required, or when old battles are resurrected, then the team's chances of being successful are diminished. Therefore, it is important that team players be provided with the skills, encouragement, and support to maximize their team contributions. And it is equally important that cross-functional team members identify and understand their individual strengths and weaknesses as team players and develop a plan to increase their effectiveness.

Being an Effective Team

A group is more than a simple collection of individuals. When a group of close friends, old enemies, or strangers comes together, something happens—the interplay, the dynamics, the leadership all combine to create a sum greater or at least different than the sum of the parts. We need to understand the dimensions of an effective cross-functional team. We then need to assess and analyze our team against those dimensions and use the analysis to build a plan to increase team effectiveness. In *Team Players and Teamwork* (1990), I created a model of an effective team that included twelve characteristics. While many of those same characteristics also apply to cross-functional teams, they play out with a different flavor in the context of a cross-functional team. There are some other dimensions that are unique to cross-functional teams. In all, there are a total of twenty factors of an effective cross-functional team. In the following chapters, I will describe each of the factors in some detail. The survey of Cross-Functional Teamwork at the end of the book includes all twenty items. You may use the survey now, to assess the effectiveness of your team at this point in time. Since the outcome of the survey is an identification of the team's strengths and weaknesses, the results may help focus your reading of the subsequent chapters.

Building Effective Interteam Relationships

No team is an island. A cross-functional team does not exist in isolation but in a constellation of other teams and key stakeholders in the organization. Hastings, Bixby, and Chaudhry-Lawton (1987) were among the first to identify "managing the outside" as a factor in successful teamwork; Ancona and Caldwell's (1990b) study of cross-functional product development teams highlighted the critical importance of boundary management. My own work with cross-functional teams tells me that the teams need to develop strong relationships with senior management, build bridges to functional department managers, fashion positive interfaces with key support groups, and successfully involve customers and suppliers. A team cannot simply be known by its own good works. Its members cannot expect others in the organization to know and care about its work as a matter of course. A cross-functional team has to, first, recognize that it needs many things that can only be provided by outsiders, such as funding, time, data, equipment, and personnel as well as ideas, encouragement, and access to key stakeholders. Second, the team needs to develop a plan that identifies the important stakeholders, common goals, relationship barriers, and ways to develop effective collaboration.

OBSTACLES TO SUCCESS

On the face of it, cross-functional teamwork looks like a great idea and an easy one to implement. Simply get together a group of people from different parts of the organization who have something to contribute about a subject and good things will happen. There is something very logical about identifying a problem and then asking eight or ten people with a variety of backgrounds, experiences, and opinions to share their ideas and develop a plan of action. But like many good theories about group behavior, when it gets tested in the field, barriers to its success emerge. In the following section, I describe the key barriers and then refer to the subsequent chapters that provide advice on how to overcome them.

Limitations of Team Leadership

While the leader plays an important role on any team, leadership of a cross-functional team is both more important and more difficult. By definition, the team is dealing with a complex subject and a diverse group of team members. The team leader has to have the technical background to understand both the subject and the contributions made by people from a wide variety of backgrounds. The team leader must also have the people management skills to facilitate the interactions of a group of people who have either had little experience working together or have had some negative experiences in working together. Few people combine high-level technical expertise with exceptional team process skills. In my experience, organizations tend to select the most logical person from a technical point of view, ignoring expertise in team dynamics. As a result, our surveys of cross-functional teams show that the major complaints about team leaders include their inability to run good meetings, involve everyone in discussions, resolve conflicts, and effectively use all of the team's human resources.

Think about the leadership of your cross-functional team; does the leader have

- The breadth of technical know-how to understand the big picture and the contributions of the broad range of team members?

- Sufficient process skills to manage the participation and involvement of team members who have a variety of past team experiences and a mixture of team player styles?

If you have some concerns about cross-functional team leaders in your organization, take a look at the suggestions in Chapter Four.

Confusion About the Team's Authority

One of the most persistent problems for cross-functional teams is their lack of empowerment. To be effective, they must have the authority to make decisions and implement them. A related obstacle is the lack of clarity about just how empowered the team really is. This confusion leads to a lack of consistency. Some teams, however — usually on the strength of the leader's skills — simply assume they have the requisite authority and therefore act in an empowered fashion. These cross-functional teams operate on the old axiom, It's easier to get forgiveness than permission. Cross-functional teams with a more conservative leadership feel the need to seek approval for every key decision and in some cases actually send up trial balloons before making recommendations, much less taking action.

Ask whether your cross-functional team

- Is clear about the team's authority to make and implement key decisions?
- Is empowered to act to the extent necessary to effectively carry out its responsibilities?

For help on addressing team empowerment issues, turn to Chapter Five.

Goal Ambiguity

Much of my work with cross-functional teams indicates a lack of a clear vision of either where they want to be or what they want to accomplish. Many teams have action items, due dates, PERT charts, and other short-term planning tools, but they often have no long-term sense of the future. Often, members of a team are clear about what pieces they themselves have to deliver but little sense of where their pieces fit into the whole. As a result, team members are committed only to making sure their deliverables are accomplished. They care little for the work of the total project or for the need to pitch in to make it work. When the team's performance is criticized by the customer, individual team members often respond with, "Well, I got my work in on time."

Assess your cross-functional team by asking,

- Does the team have clear goals that are understood and accepted by everyone? A quick test: Ask everyone to write down the team's goals, then collect and analyze the statements for both consistency and accuracy.
- To what extent were team members involved in setting team goals?
- How often does the team review the goals to both assess progress and continued relevance?

If you feel this particular barrier is impeding your team, Chapter Six can help.

Boundary Management

A team leader reported to me his disappointment that senior management had stepped in and, in a seemingly arbitrary fashion, terminated the work of his project team. When we sat down and analyzed the functioning of the team, he reluctantly admitted they had done a poor job of communicating with senior management about the work of the team. In fact, team members were just arrogant enough to feel that their individual expertise was so great that the product produced by the team would be recognized for its brilliance. The team felt that management would not fully appreciate the team's work (translation: management was not smart enough), and in addition, the team did not need any management involvement (translation: management always screws things up). In the end, it was this attitude that led to the downfall of the project because the team did a poor job of interfacing with senior management to gain its support.

Has your team taken the time to

- Identify the key stakeholders outside the team?
- Develop a plan for building positive relationships with these stakeholders?
- Assign responsibility to team members for facilitating the interfaces?

Teams lacking good stakeholder relationships will find help in Chapter Seven.

Performance Appraisal

A nagging issue, and one that is likely to increase in intensity, is that of giving team members "credit" for their performance on cross-functional teams. Many cross-functional teams take people out of their departments, but their department managers must still assess their performance; team members often complain that their work on teams does not get seriously evaluated during performance reviews. As more and more people spend more and more time serving on cross-functional teams, this will become a significant problem for organizations. I just worked with a group of technical experts whose sole responsibility was to participate on different cross-functional teams. I use the word *group* to describe them because they rarely worked together as a department team. Since their department manager rarely saw them perform — because they usually worked on teams outside the department — she could only judge them by the quality of their written work. The only way for her to get a complete view of their performance would be to obtain input from the cross-functional team leaders.

In your organization, does the performance appraisal process

- Include cross-functional team participation as a factor in an employee's appraisal?

- Require or even encourage department managers to use feedback from leaders of cross-functional teams?

See Chapter Eight for ideas on what other companies have done to overcome this barrier.

Rewards and Recognition

As more work is done with teams, organizations will have to shift the emphasis of their rewards programs from individual to team awards. At the present time, one important barrier to the success of cross-functional teams is that the focus of many awards programs is still on individual performance. While there will always be a need to recognize the individual who goes above and beyond, a good awards program must reward the collaborative efforts of teams as well. We must get away from the "star system," which rewards individuals who stand out from the crowd, and begin to reward people who help the crowd perform better. In other words, even our individual awards must acknowledge people who are effective team players — people who freely share their expertise, people who pitch in and help out when necessary, people who can effectively facilitate a meeting, and people who challenge the team to do better.

Take a look at your current rewards program:

- Does it reward individuals who are effective team players?
- Does it provide awards to teams that really demonstrate the value of collaborative efforts?

If you need ideas on team awards and recognition, you can find them in Chapter Nine.

Interpersonal Dynamics

Another persistent barrier to effective cross-functional teamwork is the failure of people to work well together in groups. Despite the increased number of people participating in recreational team sports, most people come to the workplace poorly prepared to function as a team player. Few people take courses in group dynamics and even fewer develop group process skills naturally. In comparison with functional teams, cross-functional teams are more susceptible to poor interpersonal relationships, conflicts among team members, and a lack of trust and candor. Members bring to the team their ingrained work styles developed as a result of their associations with people in their functional area. Members also bring differing priorities, past turf battles, negative attitudes about functional specialties not their own, and other baggage, all of which sets up interpersonal barriers.

In your cross-functional team, do you see

- Serious interpersonal conflicts among team members?
- A willingness to openly discuss professional and personal differences?
- Team members with the necessary interpersonal skills to facilitate good communication, effective conflict resolution, and member participation in decision making?

If these are issues for your team, Chapter Ten contains ideas on training to overcome these barriers; Chapter Twelve describes interpersonal dynamics and how to improve them.

Team Size

Many teams violate one of the fundamental principles of effective teams: Smaller is better. Just about everyone knows intuitively what researchers have proven over and over again about the size of a team—about four to six members, but certainly no more than ten members, works best. Yet cross-functional teams continue to try to operate with teams of twenty-five, thirty-five, and even fifty members. In fact, cross-functional teams seem especially willing to increase their membership rosters to a number that ultimately makes them unwieldy and ineffective. There seems to be a drive to involve as many people as possible as if, in some peculiar way, large membership is an indicator of successful teamwork. Paradoxically, a large membership is likely to be an impediment instead. In some organizations, many unnecessary people are invited to join the team because it is assumed that they would be offended if they were overlooked. Quite the contrary—they would be delighted to have one less meeting to attend and one less responsibility to worry about.

Take a hard look at the membership of your team:

- Are there simply too many people on the team; could you do just as well or better with fewer members?

- If the membership is large, do you use a core team to make key decisions? Do you break down into working committees to accomplish most of the real work?

If your team is too large, go to Chapter Eleven for ideas on how to deal with size.

Lack of Management Support

There is very little a team can accomplish without the support of management, both senior management and functional department management. This is often the "killer" barrier; the team can overcome many of the other barriers by team actions, such as training, good leadership, planning, and communication; but if key management stakeholders either do not cooperate or, worse, sabotage the team, there is little that the team can do about it. Effective boundary management can only go so far.

In your organization,

- Does senior management have a clear goal of supporting and encouraging cross-functional teamwork?
- Do functional department managers understand the priorities of cross-functional teams in relation to the managers' own departments?

Senior managers can refer to Chapter Thirteen for advice on how to build a team-based culture in the organization.

In this chapter we have looked at team and organizational barriers to successful cross-functional teamwork. In the chapters that follow we look at each of these barriers and suggest specific methods for overcoming them.

4

Leading
Cross-Functional Teams

In recent years, much has been written and discussed about leadership. Various people have emphasized visionary leadership, shared leadership, empowered leadership, and even charismatic leadership. Leaders of cross-functional teams must possess all of these characteristics and more. It's a tough job.

Leaders of cross-functional teams must manage a diverse group of people who often have a wide variety of backgrounds, training, and interests. In addition to people management skills, a team leader must also be able to follow the often highly technical nature of a team's work. Frequently, he or she must accomplish all of this without the authority that is usually associated with a leadership position in a functional organization.

So there you have it. Your job as leader of a cross-functional team is to manage a group of people from different departments or functions who have little experience in working together and, given the choice, would probably choose not to work together. You will be given little or no authority over their performance but you will nevertheless be held accountable for the success of the team. You must have sufficient knowledge of the team's task to follow the discussions and reports. And you should have the group process skills to facilitate the participation of team members, resolve conflicts, and gain a consensus on key issues.

Given this job description, few people would apply. Even fewer would be able to meet these standards. As I said, it's a tough job, but it must be done. Cross-functional teams are increasing and the need for leaders is on the rise.

Some people have mistakenly compared the position of general or plant manager to the position of cross-functional team leader. A plant manager, for example, does have a diverse set of people representing different functions reporting to him or her: production manager, maintenance superintendent, manager of engineering, director of labor relations, and several others. However, these managers are rarely the head of a team in the sense of a group of people with a clearly defined purpose of their own (as distinguished from the plant's objectives) and the need to produce a joint work product. Typically, the people in the plant consist of working groups, in which the sum total of their individual efforts is sufficient to meet the plant's objectives. As Katzenbach and Smith (1993a) found in their examination of teamwork in thirty companies, top management teams "need little time to shape their purpose since the leader usually establishes it. Meetings are run against well prioritized agendas. And decisions are implemented through individual assignments and accountabilities" (p. 118). Good solid management techniques are sufficient for this type of group leader because the authority of the leader and the goals of the team are clear and unequivocal. However, cross-functional teams of the sort described in Chapter Two require a new brand of leadership. (As an aside, there would be nothing wrong with the working group in a plant becoming a team by developing a set of team objectives and interdependent member tasks.)

A NEW BREED OF LEADER

At the present time and in most cases, "the professional hierarchy does dictate the selection of the team leader — the physician in primary medical settings, the educator in school settings — but unfortunately, these individuals, whether by training or temperament, may not be the person best suited for team leadership" (Pearson, 1983, p. 394). The most logical person from a task or subject-matter perspective may not be the best person to lead a cross-functional team.

Many technically trained professionals lack the experience of working effectively in groups. In fact, they often chose their profession because it involved working independently with minimal supervision and interpersonal contact. The doctor, the engineer, the computer scientist, and many other professionals who may prefer to work alone or with limited corporate interference must now lead teams of people with different backgrounds.

Simply appointing the smartest physician or electrical engineer to head a project team does not ensure success. The key to the success of these teams is the ability to meld the talents of this diverse group. Our data show that the people typically selected to lead these teams tend to be task-oriented team players, whom I call Contributors (Parker, 1990). Contributors tend to be excellent at getting the team to focus on the immediate task in an organized and efficient manner. They emphasize short-term, specific outcomes with a great concern for the quality of the product. The strengths of the Contributors are sometimes offset by a failure to have a vision and to set long-term goals. And they usually do not see the value of positive group process, which consists of a concern for good interpersonal relationships, effective involvement by team members, open communication, conflict resolution, and consensus decision making. Some companies are beginning to recognize the importance of good process skills to the success of cross-functional teams. In one recent case, a drug development team in a pharmaceutical company was falling behind schedule to bring an important new compound to the market. The company replaced the team leader, a highly trained physician, with a scientist who had the interpersonal skills to pull the group together; the team subsequently beat the original milestones for submitting a new drug application.

Group Process Skills

The successful leader of a cross-functional team must have the necessary technical expertise to understand the issues and keep the team focused on the goal. Many team leaders are able to meet this requirement. However, while an understanding of the technical issues is necessary, it is not sufficient to ensure the success of the team. The successful leader is also able to understand and facilitate the human dynamics of the team — what I call providing positive process leadership. Process leadership involves bringing together the strangers who are working together for the first time, the colleagues who have worked together on other tasks, and the enemies who have been on opposite sides in past organizational battles.

Some of these positive process skills include

- Asking questions that bring out ideas and stimulate discussion

- Using paraphrasing and other listening skills to ensure effective communication

- Managing group discussions to encourage quiet members to participate and talkative members to adhere to limits

- Establishing an informal, relaxed climate where members feel free to candidly express their points of view

- Using the consensus method to reach decisions on key team issues

- Involving members in the setting of goals and objectives
- Implementing good team meeting guidelines, including agenda planning and time management
- Insisting that team members respect each other and that each person's contribution is valued
- Identifying and dealing with team members' dysfunctional behaviors
- Celebrating the achievement of milestones and other team accomplishments
- Using recognition methods, task assignments, and other techniques to motivate team members

Leadership Empowerment

Another key requirement is the ability to work in an environment where you are expected to have a great deal of responsibility with little or at best murky authority. The challenge for the team leader is to either clarify the team's authority or act as if he or she has been empowered. Many a team leader has become frustrated with his or her inability to control the resources on the team. The point is that the leader cannot control or manage the people on the team—he or she has to *lead* them. As Sheila Mello, vice president of BBN Communications in Cambridge, Massachusetts, and a team leader herself put it: "Team members have their own functional managers, so I cannot tell them what to do" (Whiting, 1991, p. 54). See Chapter Five for more on empowerment.

Goal Setting

Effective leadership also involves setting a direction for the team. Setting goals is of course important to the success of any team. However, it appears to be especially critical to the success of cross-functional teams. My colleague, Ira Asherman, a New York–based consultant to the pharmaceutical industry, points out that the failure to set goals is one of the most persistent criticisms of leaders of project teams who are responsible for bringing new drugs to the market. In addition to the typical reasons for having team goals, leaders of cross-functional teams are able to use the goals to resolve conflicts among members and obtain needed resources from important stakeholders. For example, Pearson (1983) points out that the inevitable conflicts that emerge among professionals on inter-disciplinary child assessment teams can be resolved more easily if the team has "agreed on common goals" (p. 395). See Chapter Six for a discussion of team goals.

Flexibility

Flexibility is another key characteristic of the effective leader of a cross-functional team. A rigid, highly structured person who likes to have lots of clear rules and regulations will have great difficulty in this environment. Cross-functional teams operate in a fluid, changing arena. As hard as we try to clarify authority, establish policies, and publish manuals, the day-to-day functioning of the team will be changeable. Team leaders must be prepared to react and adapt with ease.

Resolving Conflict

One of the most important process skills is the ability to resolve conflict. We assume there will be some conflict on a cross-functional team. In fact, it is a given, even encouraged. It is the diversity of ideas, expertise, and styles that is the very strength of a cross-functional team. However, a strength can turn into a weakness if it is not handled with skill. First, the effective leader needs to understand that conflict is not bad; disagreements on the team are to be expected. Viewed from a different perspective, if there is total agreement throughout the life of the team, there is something wrong. Either we don't have a diverse membership or the diversity exists but is being suppressed or smoothed over. The effective leader encourages the expression of opinion, helps the team look at both sides of issues, forms subgroups to study problems, keeps the team goals and the customer in view, and uses the consensus method to make key team decisions. However, beyond the internal dynamics issues such as goal setting, conflict resolution, and empowerment, the effective leader must also address a series of external factors.

Stakeholder Relationships

It is virtually impossible for a cross-functional team to focus exclusively on the internal operation of the team. Even with the best technical work and group process, the team will fail if it is unable to work effectively with key stakeholders outside the team. Stakeholders may run the gamut from the directors of functional departments represented on the team, to upper management (which funds and supports the work), to government agencies that influence or approve the work, to community groups whose members care about the team's work, to other departments in the company that will make, sell, or service the team's product. The team leader is often the key facilitator of the interactions with the team's stakeholders. This function requires good communications skills, such as listening, negotiating, and resolving conflict. See Chapter Seven for ideas on how to build effective stakeholder relationships.

Obtaining Resources

Jane Perlmutter, a manager with Bell Communications Research, suggests that the effective leader of a cross-functional team in telecommunications is able to "simply get team members what they need, when they need it" (interview with the author, January 1993). The needs of team members vary widely, from laboratory time, computer support, and the development of prototypes, to less tangible items such as fast turnarounds on approvals, freeing up of team members' time to allow them to work on team projects, and recognition for team members' accomplishments. In some cases, getting the team what it needs may mean additional human resources in the form of experts to help team members understand an issue or solve a knotty problem. Effective team leaders have "to be tenacious and want to make things happen . . . and they must be willing to make noise at the top and ask embarrassing questions when obstacles arise," according to Theresa Pratt, a team leader at Codex Corporation, an electronics company in Mansfield, Massachusetts (Whiting, 1991, p. 54). The effective leader knows how to "work" the system to get the team what it needs to get the job done.

Orchestrating Communications

Sometimes what the team needs is simply to be left alone. Team members do not want outsiders, including and especially top management, poking around. The team needs time to work on the problem or do some development work unencumbered by the need to make progress reports, answer questions, or deliver presentations. The effective team leader runs "interference" for the team by providing upper management and other stakeholders with enough information to satisfy their curiosity while keeping the team insulated. In other situations, as Geri Weber of Bell Communications Research notes, the liaison role of the team leader involves obtaining systematic feedback from management (interview with the author, January 1993).

Cross-functional teams need to know that management supports the project; therefore, the teams want regular feedback from their management sponsors. Since it is often difficult to get top managers to come to team meetings, it's up to the team leader to communicate with these managers about the team's work, get their reactions, and report back to the team. In the electronics industry, which makes heavy use of cross-functional teams, "the team leader is a communicator, serving as the project's main point of contact between the company's executive ranks and the [team]" (Whiting, 1991, p. 54). (More on boundary management in Chapter Seven.)

LEADERSHIP ALTERNATIVES

As organizations understand the difficulty of identifying effective leaders for their cross-functional teams, they are looking for alternative solutions. There are a number of possibilities.

Coleadership

One approach being tried in a number of places is co-leadership. When there is a natural division of responsibility, this approach makes sense. One division of leadership roles that may work is the splitting of technical and process leadership functions. In this model, the technical or scientific expert (for example, the engineer or physician) focuses on the task while someone with experience in group dynamics or team management addresses the process issues.

Facilitation Support

Some organizations provide the team leader with a trained facilitator to help run the team. In this model, there is one team leader, usually a technical guru, backed up by a human resources staff person or other professional with good group process skills. The facilitator helps the team leader prepare for the meeting, offers advice and coaching on process issues, intervenes as necessary during team meetings, and works with individual team members outside the meetings.

Project Manager as Team Leader

Some organizations opt for a professional project manager to serve as team leader. This approach simply bypasses the technical leader in favor of a trained project manager. It's felt that the technical and scientific input can be provided by the members of the team.

Rotating Team Leaders

This model applies to long-term projects that have a series of key phases. The leader changes as the project moves into a new phase; the new leader comes from the function that carries the ball during that particular phase. As a result, the leader is the person most knowledgeable about the current work of the team. It also means that the leadership burden is shared, and it often means that the various phase leaders support each other.

Leadership Training

This approach simply says that every cross-functional team leader needs solid leadership training. The training tends to focus on the group process aspects of the position because these skills are usually the least well developed. See Chapter Ten for ideas on team leader training.

LEADERSHIP REQUIREMENTS FOR CROSS-FUNCTIONAL TEAMS

Effective leadership is effective leadership. There are some universal truths that cut across types of teams. There are some common characteristics of effective team leaders that apply to all types of teams — self-directed work teams, top management planning teams, temporary task forces, quality action teams, committees, and plain old-fashioned business teams. Effective leaders have a clear vision and are able to communicate that vision to the members of the team. They develop a sense of urgency about the team's work, involve team members in goal setting and decision making, and foster a climate of openness and honesty. People want to work for them — they have, dare we say it, charisma! Beyond these common characteristics, however, leaders of cross-functional teams need more. The unique features of a cross-functional team call for some additional, special characteristics or a different spin on some familiar qualities.

The most significant leadership requirements for cross-functional team leadership include:

1. A working knowledge of the technical issues being addressed by the team. A *working* knowledge does not mean being the smartest person but rather someone who is able to clearly follow the work of the team.

2. Experience and skills in managing group process issues. *Process management* means an ability to facilitate team member participation, conflict resolution, and consensus building.

3. An ability to work with little, no, or unclear authority. The effective leader often has to act as if he or she is empowered.

4. A willingness and the relevant skills to "manage the outside." The effective leader must develop ongoing relationships with key stakeholders in other parts of the organizations. Key stakeholders include the leaders of functional departments represented on the team, senior management sponsors of the team, and resource people who provide the team with various types of support and services.

5. The know-how to help the team establish a mission and set goals and objectives. Clear direction helps team members balance their responsibilities to the team and their functional departments.

6. The knowledge and assertiveness to obtain the necessary resources for the team. The effective leader pushes and pulls the organization to get those tangible and intangible resources that the team needs to succeed.

7. The ability to protect the team from undue and counterproductive outside interference. The effective leader "stands guard"—fending off people who may want to interfere with, control, or unduly influence the work of the team.

8. A willingness to change and adapt as conditions change and the needs of the team evolve. The effective leader must be flexible.

9. A sense of humor. People from different areas, colleagues, strangers, and others can unite in an informal, relaxed atmosphere that includes good-natured kidding ("All you engineers want to do is . . ."), social banter ("Did

you hear what happened at the Phillies game last . . . ?"), and company gossip ("At the senior management re-treat . . ."). Effective leaders take the work but not them-selves seriously.

IT'S A TOUGH JOB

Leaders of cross-functional teams have a difficult job because it requires pulling together a group of people who may be close friends, archenemies, or simply strangers. It requires dealing with upper management, functional department heads, sup-port groups, and other stakeholders who may or may not support the team's goal. The keys to success are (1) select the right person based on the criteria suggested in this chapter, and (2) provide training and support on an ongoing basis.

In the next chapter, one of the most difficult issues for team leaders is discussed — empowerment. For the leader, it often comes down to, How do you get things done when you are not in charge?

5

Empowering Teams to Do the Job

One of the most important and often frustrating aspects of cross-functional teams is the authority of the team. Dare we use the E-word to discuss the authority of a cross-functional team? While it conjures up all sorts of negative images and cries of "just another management fad" or the "topic du jour," empowerment describes a critical issue for teams. The most effective and happiest teams are fully empowered. What does this mean? An empowered team is one that has both the responsibility and authority to carry out its mission; it exercises ownership and control over its task and process. In a practical sense, it means a group of people who make decisions about their own work without checking with anyone. However, it is important to understand that teams migrate to this position over time. It does not just happen one day, when you are suddenly "empowered." At one plant where I worked, some team members and supervisors mistakenly felt that once the team training course was completed, they were empowered. Somehow, graduation was equated with empowerment. Later, it was explained that the transfer of decision-making authority takes place over time. In fact, it may take up to eighteen months for a team to reach the stage of full empowerment.

REAL-TIME EMPOWERMENT

Lack of empowerment or confusion about the team's authority causes problems. Turf battles among team members can stymie a team's progress. Consider this scenario:

> In 1990, Becton Dickinson developed a new instrument called the Bactec 860, designed to process blood samples. A team leader was assigned and immediately put together a project team of engineers, marketers, manufacturers, and suppliers. While the group eventually launched the Bactec 860 some 25 percent faster than its previous best efforts, [CEO Raymond] Gilmartin wasn't satisfied. There was still too much time-wasting debate between marketing and engineering over product specifications. . . . Marketing argued that Bactec needed more features to please the customer, while engineering countered that the features would take too long to design and be too costly. Further inquiry led management to the nub of the problem: because the team leader reported to the head of engineering, he didn't have sufficient clout to resolve the conflict between the two sides. Today the company makes sure all its team leaders have access to a division head, which gives them the authority to settle disputes between different functions [Dumaine, 1991, p. 42].

In response to its large and growing number of managed health care customers, a major pharmaceutical company established a market planning team composed of top-level marketers from its key product lines. The managed-care customers were demanding a coordinated corporate offering and a single point of contact for dealing with the company. While the marketing representatives on the team recognized the necessity of cross-functional teamwork to respond to the needs of these customers, their bosses did not buy into the concept. As a result, after investing considerable effort in developing business plans for each major account, the team died. Good idea, customer focus, technical support, but no authority to act.

On the other hand, when cross-functional teams are empowered to act, great things happen. In some organizations, empowerment means the freedom to act with minimal reporting and accounting restrictions and the flexibility to work around the system. In organizations where rapid response time is valued, and in fact produces value, eliminating excessive approvals is equated with empowerment. And it works. At Calgon Corporation, Frank Daniher, director of water management research and development, reported that a cross-functional team, with the freedom and flexibility to respond quickly to customer demands, was able to cut the time it takes to commercialize a new polymer from twelve to four months (Wolff, 1988). Finn Knudsen, director of research and development for the Adolph Coors Company, said that a team composed of people from research, marketing, sales, production scheduling, production, quality control and assurance, and packaging was able to cut by 50 percent the time it usually takes to launch a new product. The new product, Winterfest, a seasonal beer, was driven by a cross-functional team that was empowered by top management to do whatever it took to get the product to the market in time for the Christmas holiday season (Wolff, 1988).

The well-known story of AT&T's development of the cordless phone known as the 4200 also demonstrates the success of a cross-functional team empowered to act. John Hanley, vice president of product development, "formed teams of six to 12, including engineers, manufacturers, and marketers, with authority to make every decision on how the product would work, look, be made, and cost. The key was to set rigid speed requirements—six weeks, say, for freezing all design specs. Because the team didn't need to send each decision up the line for approval, it could meet these strict deadlines. With this new approach AT&T cut development time for the 4200 phone from two years to just a year while lowering costs and increasing quality" (Dumaine, 1989, p. 57).

In another part of the AT&T giant, empowered teams have turned the organization around. AT&T Credit Corporation (ATTCC), which provides financing for people who lease AT&T equipment, set up regional teams of people who handle the total business, from processing applications to credit checks to contracts and collections (Hoerr, 1989). With managers offering advice only, the teams make decisions on dealing with customers, setting up work schedules, and even hiring new employees. The results: The number of leases processed daily has more than doubled, and decision time on an application has been reduced from forty-eight to twenty-four hours. All this empowerment goes right to the bottom line, because ATTCC is growing at a 40 to 50 percent compound rate.

At BSD, a software inventory control firm, empowered multidisciplinary teams are the key to the company's success (Belasco, 1991). The teams are organized around a specific customer or set of customers. Each team includes all the necessary sales, service, and technical experts to support a given customer. These teams are responsible for making all decisions on how to best serve their customer, including the training and development of their own team. James Belasco, a consultant to the company, reports that empowerment is working to make BSD "one of the most profitable businesses of its kind" (interview with the author, January 1993).

Empowered teams are also having a positive impact on buyer-seller relationships, where cross-functional teams integrate cross-technological components. "For example, a new automobile brake, which combines traditional metallurgical and mechanical engineering with advanced electronics and microcomputer technologies, requires the integration of departments and personnel that have never worked together before" (Lyons, Krachenberg, and Henke, 1990, p. 30). These cross-functional teams make all the decisions about the product involved, including the selection of vendors. A core team from six different departments join with purchasing to manage the total process. Other functional specialties, including at times supplier representatives, augment the team.

EMPOWERMENT: HOW TO GET IT

Empowerment Is Not a Gift

There are two aspects to the empowerment issue: (1) the degree of clarity about the authority of the team and (2) the extent of the team's authority. Many cross-functional teams are set up without any thought given to the degree of authority delegated to the team. In other cases, authority is given to the team but the team simply does not use it. They just don't believe it. However, many cross-functional teams were never intended to be empowered teams. And yet because this was never clarified, the team members wander around frustrated by what they perceive as their ineffectiveness.

The first thing to understand is that team empowerment is not a gift. A team cannot be given real, operating authority as a present from senior management. Real empowerment — just like motivation — comes from within the team. The members act as if they are empowered. Bill Hines, an executive director with Bell Communications Research (Bellcore) in New Jersey, spent almost a year working on a policy statement that empowers project managers (and their cross-functional teams) to make key decisions about project costs, deliverables, and resource allocation based on customer needs. Although all the right words are down on paper and the policy statement has been approved by top management, as Hines puts it, "Now the trick is get someone to stick a toe in the water and make a decision that benefits the customer but reduces the head count of a line manager" (interview with the author, January 1993). This is not to denigrate the importance of a clear policy statement on empowerment. Such a written document is an important first step in the process, but it cannot stand alone. The policy must be buttressed by statements and actions by senior management. Cross-functional teams must continually hear the message that they are empowered to act as long as it is in the best interests of the organization.

Teams must also see actions that reinforce the written policy and verbal remarks. They must see senior management keeping a hands-off position in regard to cross-functional teams. For example, one of the fastest ways to unempower a team is to second-guess or, worse, change a decision made by the team because a functional department manager complained. As a director with a Fortune 100 company told me, "Around here, the authority of our project teams is, at best, ambiguous. We are told 'you can make decisions.' But, in reality, if senior management doesn't like it, it won't fly."

How Teams Get Empowered

1. *Empowered teams act empowered.* They take responsibility and assume they have the authority to act. They do not wait for top management's approval. Jim Kochanski, director of human resources for Northern Telecom in Research Triangle Park, North Carolina, says that the question he hears often from leaders of cross-functional teams is, "'How do I get the right kind of commitment, behavior, and decisions out of them if I don't have straight-line authority over them?' What they probably mean is, 'if I don't have the authority to fire them'" (interview with the author, January 1993). Kochanski uses that statement to facilitate a discussion of what you can do instead to become empowered or to act as if you are empowered to get what you need done. He also uses the statement to challenge the assumption that straight-line authority always works. The focus has to be on taking action rather than waiting for someone else to make it happen for you.

2. *Empowered teams have a clear focus.* You can't ask for empowerment unless you can answer the question, for what? or, to do what? No one is going to give you carte blanche empowerment like a line of credit. You need to be clear what you want to do — your vision or mission should be clear to you. In fact, when you have an inspiring goal, you are likely to move forward as if you are empowered. An engaging vision or a challenging goal will move team members to action. It creates its own empowerment. Chapter Six discusses the importance of goals for a team composed of colleagues, antagonists, and strangers.

3. *Empowered teams engage key stakeholders.* While empowered teams are free to act, they do so in concert with key stakeholders in the organizations. Cross-functional teams need, first and foremost, the support of the functional department managers. As survey respondent Barbara Bennett of The Stanley Works put it, "While cross-functional teams have the responsibility to solve problems and implement solutions, they must get the right stakeholders involved." Bellcore's Bill Hines, who has given a great deal of thought to this area, believes strongly that "cross-functional teams will fail if they don't (1) have all interested parties involved and (2) do the stakeholdering upfront to gain agreement that this is an issue we need to work on and that we will all be part of the solution" (interview with the author, January 1993). Since so much of the work done by cross-functional teams involves coordination with other teams in the organization, their support is critical. Empowerment does not mean ramming your decisions through the organization.

4. *Empowered teams are committed.* The members of the team must all care deeply about the team's purpose and be ready to work hard to achieve it. This is especially true for cross-functional teams because the members come from different areas in the organization, each with his or her own set of prior commitments. Members need to put aside these often conflicting commitments and get behind an overarching team challenge.

As an exercise, ask team members to recall a team they

thought was successful and to describe what made it successful. More often than not, deep commitment will be on their list of success factors. It really doesn't matter what team members rally around. It can be, as Northern Telecom Jim Kochanski points out, "a common enemy, like a competitor." In the cases of Calgon and Coors, the rallying point was the challenge of bringing a quality product to the market in record time (Wolff, 1988). Paul Allaire, Xerox's CEO, puts it another way: "You can't get people to focus on the bottom line. You have to give them an objective like 'satisfy the customer' that everybody can relate to. It's the only way to break down those barriers and get people from different functions working together" (Dumaine, 1991, p. 42).

NOT ALL TEAMS ARE EMPOWERED EQUALLY

It is useful to look at the empowerment of cross-functional teams on a continuum. In practice, teams can experience varying degrees of authority in their day-to-day operations. It can be frustrating for a team to be told or to believe that it is fully empowered when in fact it is not. Since the E-word is bandied about a great deal nowadays, it is not surprising that this confusion occurs. Therefore, it can be useful for a team to analyze its actions and especially its decisions against a model of cross-functional team empowerment.

Empowerment Factors

There are a number of factors that have an impact on the degree of team empowerment. These factors also help team members understand where their team falls on the empowerment continuum (see Table 5.1 and Figure 5.1). We have identified three major points on the continuum: Coordinating, Semiempowered, and Empowered. Coordinating teams are task forces, committees, and some quality teams that are

Table 5.1. Factors in the Empowerment Continuum
of Cross-Functional Teams.

	Type of Team		
Factors	Coordinating	Semiempowered	Empowered
Members	Part-time	Part-/Full-time	Full-time
Leaders	Part-time	Part-/Full-time	Full-time
Leader's Role	Check Schedules	Coaching, Facilitating	Empowering Members
Resource Control	Limited	Great Influence	Control
Mission	Set by Senior Management	Set by Senior Management	Set by Team
Task Focus	Limited	Great	Total
Performance Appraisal	Functional Manager	Functional Manager	Team/Team Leader
Company Policy	Followed Closely	Stretched	Work Around/ Ignore
Colocation	Rarely	Often	Usually
Final Decisions	Recommend	Great Influence	Control

set up to develop recommendations, produce a report, or solve a specific problem. Their product is then presented to top management for approval. Semiempowered teams are often aspiring self-directed teams in the early stages or project teams that, while they have considerable influence, still must get approval for major decisions. Fully empowered teams are just that—they control their resources, set their goals, develop their plans, and then make and implement their decisions.

Members. The members of an empowered cross-functional team are usually full-time members of the team. This is their only job. It may be temporary but it is full-time for the duration of the project. When team members of fully empowered project teams have other jobs, it makes commitment and therefore success more difficult to achieve. When members of your team

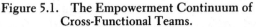

**Figure 5.1.   The Empowerment Continuum of
Cross-Functional Teams.**

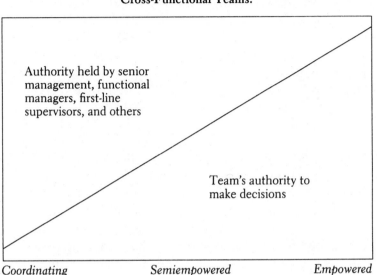

Authority held by senior
management, functional
managers, first-line
supervisors, and others

Team's authority to
make decisions

Coordinating   *Semiempowered*   *Empowered*

are also members of three and four other teams, as is the case
in most pharmaceutical project teams, it sometimes sets up
competing interests. Bill Hines of Bellcore told me he strongly
believes in getting people out of their jobs for certain periods
of time to work on a project. "Some past efforts have failed,"
Hines says, "because members were told, 'This is a part-time
effort and you do it whenever you have time,'" (interview with
the author, January 1993). There should be no hard and fast
rule that says empowered teams are composed of only full-
time members. However, as one person told me, "They should
act as if this is their only job."

      However, a great deal of good work is done by teams with
members who are part-time but who have the support of their
managers to participate on the team. The capability of these
teams to coordinate activities and offer recommendations for
the solution of important problems is significant. Some cross-
functional teams were never intended to be fully empowered.
They were established as vehicles for what I call "coordination" of the work of various functions in the organization or to
get input from different experts on a specific problem.

Leaders.   In much the same way, leaders of fully empowered cross-functional teams tend to be assigned on a full-time basis, whereas in most self-directed teams in factories and offices, team leaders also perform their regular job (for example, production operator, claims representative). However, some cross-functional teams are led by people who not only have other jobs but serve on other teams as well. As leaders more fully commit their time to a team, the team tends to increase in its level of empowerment.

Leader's Role.   The role of the leader differs as you move up the empowerment continuum. The leader of a task force charged with coordinating the work of various functions or the leader of a quality action team usually sees his or her job as checking to make sure that action items are completed or certain reports are submitted. The role of a coordinating team leader is to ensure that the team prepares and submits a set of recommendations or a proposal for upper management's approval. The leader's role in an empowered cross-functional team is either to make the decisions or to coach and facilitate the team to make its own decisions.

Resource Control.   One of the key issues is who controls the team's resources and its access to additional resources. Empowered teams have, within reason, the ability to get what they need in order to do the job. Resources may include equipment, tools, and machinery as well as people. If the resources are outside the organization, empowered teams are free to deal directly with suppliers. For example, at the Texas plant of a major health care company, cross-functional teams are told, "You know what you need to do, so just do it. If you need help from management to make it happen, let us know." As the human resource manager put it, "We've turned these teams loose and said go for it" (interview with the author, February 1993). However, he also points out that there are regular review meetings, so that senior management knows what the teams are doing and has an opportunity to comment on their work. He characterizes these cross-functional teams as "semiempowered." On the other hand, teams with coordinating responsibility and therefore little authority must seek approval for changes or additions to the team's resource base.

Mission.   Teams with little authority are usually handed their mission by senior management. They are told what is expected of them in the way of output, although they may have the opportunity to shape the goals and the plan for implementation. Empowered teams are usually able to establish their own mission, goals, and implementation plan as long as they are in line with the corporate vision. Falling somewhere in between on the continuum are cross-functional teams at the health care company referred to in the previous section. They are handed a technical problem (for example, the reliability of diagnostic equipment) and told to run with it until they come up with a solution or recommendations.

Task Focus.   Empowered cross-functional teams are usually highly focused on the group's task and committed to work hard to produce a quality product. Since team members are dedicated on a full-time basis to the team, their energy is concentrated on the team's task. But other teams whose members may have other responsibilities have a less-concentrated focus. Many a team leader of a coordinating team has heard team members say, "I just couldn't get that data in time for this meeting because of other priorities."

Performance Appraisal.   The level of the commitment of team members is often a function of who does their performance appraisal—because the person or organization responsible for the appraisal usually gets most of their attention and effort. In cross-functional teams with full-time members, the responsibility is clear—the team leader or other team members conduct the appraisal process. (See Chapter Eight for a discussion of team appraisals.) As you go down the continuum to the less empowered teams, it is the functional manager or boss of the team member who handles the employee's appraisal.

Company Policy.   Effective cross-functional teams that are fully empowered to act are also usually empowered (or their members feel empowered) to stretch, work around, or ignore formal company policy. For example, the product development teams that are trying to speed up the process often ignore the existing approval requirements; they try to work around procedures that bog down development and make no business sense. Coordinating teams tend to follow the rules because they do not want to run the risk of angering the very people who will be reviewing their proposals and perhaps have input into their performance appraisal.

Colocation.   Working in the same building, on the same floor, and in the same area is often considered a plus for effective teamwork. It is even more important for cross-functional teams but sometimes more difficult to pull off because members may be scattered. Physical proximity promotes collaboration. Simply being able to go into the next office or laboratory to discuss a problem, or having lunch together, or just schmoozing in the hallway breaks down the discipline and style barriers that are inherent in a cross-functional team because of its diverse membership. Empowered teams are more often housed in the same building either because the value of regular interaction is recognized or team members were already working in the same area. Semiempowered and coordinating teams are much less likely to be colocated because it is not perceived to be important. However, some of these teams may be colocated simply because they were formerly all housed in the same building. See Chapter Twelve for more discussion of colocation as a factor in promoting positive team dynamics.

Final Decisions.   By definition, an empowered team has the authority to make decisions that stick. Semiempowered teams usually have the ability to exert great influence on final decisions. The final decision is usually based on a recommendation from the team, and if the team has been doing good advance work with the key stakeholders, its recommendation will be tantamount to the final decision. In effect, the team will operate as if it were fully empowered.

That's Empowerment!

In the end, a diverse group of people coming together on a cross-functional team will be effective to the extent that they agree on a common goal, set aside their individual department priorities, develop a plan to reach that goal and then commit to work together to attain it. That's empowerment! The next chapter shows you how to take the first step—setting a clear goal.

6

Setting Goals
for Shared
Commitments

The essence of a team is common commitment.
Without it, groups perform as individuals;
with it, they become a powerful unit
of collective performance.
Jon Katzenbach and Douglas K. Smith
(1993a, p. 112)

It might seem as if I'm stating the obvious to say that an effective team needs to have a clear set of goals. If it's true that all teams must have a common purpose, what's so special about cross-functional teams? All teams do need to have a clear mission and a set of goals that everyone on the team supports. But because cross-functional teams are different from other types of teams, goal setting is even more critical to their success. After observing many project meetings and surveying hundreds of team members in the pharmaceutical industry, management consultant Ira Asherman points out that "clear, overarching goals is one of the most important factors that distinguish the high-performing (cross-functional) drug development teams" (interview with the author, January 1993). Members may come to the team as strangers, or know each other only informally, or have had some past negative experiences on teams. A solid goal-setting process culminating in a clear mission and set of goals can reduce conflicts and build positive relationships.

GOALS REDUCE CONFLICTS

One of the most important roles that clear goals play on a cross-functional team is to reduce the potential for conflicts and minimize past differences among the various disciplines represented on the team. Even without any past differences, people often come to a team with a belief that the contribution of their function is the most important and should take precedence over the other areas, or have more clout in the decision-making process or in resource allocation. Sometimes the assumed rank order of the various disciplines is embedded in the existing culture of the organization.

Therefore, team members bring these beliefs to the cross-functional team. For example, in child development teams — which bring together professionals in a variety of disciplines to provide assessments of children with developmental disabilities — Paul Pearson, past president of the American Academy for Cerebral Palsy and Developmental Medicine, found that "human nature and training dictate that each professional will tend to see his own area as representing one of the most important goals, if not the main one. The orthopedic surgeon may see ambulation as the paramount goal; the psychologist is most concerned about the child's psychosocial development; the educator is certain that nothing should interfere with the child being educated adequately; while the parents may be most concerned that the child learns activities or skills of daily living" (Pearson, 1983, p. 391).

The resolution of these differences is facilitated by the development of a common goal, which all members of the team accept and are willing to support. As Pearson points out, it has to be more specific than simply "we are all interested in the welfare of the child" (p. 391). Although cross-functional teams often start out with general goals — such as to improve

quality, satisfy the customer, improve market share, or decrease turnaround time—they must quickly move to something more specific and operational. Many teams are given a
broad charter by senior management. The team then must
come up with a clear mission and set of goals, which it in turn
transmits to senior management and the functional department heads.

GOALS BUILD PARTNERSHIPS

Not only do goals help cross-functional teams resolve inter-
group conflicts, they also help maintain positive relationships
with the functional departments and senior management.
At Reader's Digest, a company that ranks high on Fortune's
list of America's Most Admired Corporations, top management scopes out an issue and then hands it off to a cross-
functional team to "work out the details," according to Naomi
Marrow, the company's director of human resources (interview with the author, January 1993). Team members have to
buy into the overall goal (for example, reducing customer
complaints, "globalizing" the business), help fashion a team
goal that is more specific, and then get the support of their
functional departments. In turn, the functional departments
have to adjust their goals to the overall team goal or alert the
team and/or management to potential difficulties or conflicts
in priorities. In this way, the teams at Reader's Digest address
one of the major barriers to the success of a cross-functional
team—lack of support by the functional departments.

A similar approach is used at Pacific Bell by Jose Verger, a
product manager who works with cross-functional teams responsible for the development of major new telecommunications products and services. "You have to be clear about your
vision," Verger says, "and then communicate that vision to the
team" (interview with the author, January 1993). With Verger
playing facilitator, the team tries to assess the degree of the
problem's complexity, develop a series of objectives, and ulti-

mately, set a very specific time line of milestones. This process, Verger says, builds support for his vision because functional department managers are clear about the team's priorities. Later, when a department balks at supplying the assistance it promised, he can refer to the team's goals and milestones. Goals break down barriers between enemies and strangers and help build positive relationships.

GOAL-SETTING
TECHNIQUES FOR
CROSS-FUNCTIONAL TEAMS

Make Goals Specific

Xerox, which makes heavy use of cross-functional teams to solve all sorts of problems, begins with a broad problem, often emanating from a customer, and then turns it over to a team. For example, several years ago, customers said what they really wanted Xerox to be able to tell them was when their new copier would arrive, be installed, and up and running (Dumaine, 1991). Unfortunately at the time, Xerox could not give them this information with any degree of accuracy. CEO Paul Allaire turned the problem over to an experienced middle manager, who put together a cross-functional team from distribution, accounting, and sales. The team set its objective as satisfying the customer's need to know; as a result, the team developed a tracking system that follows each copier through the distribution process.

Motorola's Communications Sector provides another example of the value of a clear mission followed by the articulation of specific objectives and plans by a cross-functional team. Composed of representatives from industrial engineering, robotics, process engineering, procurement, product design, human resources, and finance, and a vendor representative from Hewlett-Packard, the cross-functional team was charged with developing "an automated, on-shore, profitable production operation for its high-volume Bravo pager line" (Clark and Wheelwright, 1992, p. 14). Known as the Bandit Team (because team members would "take" ideas from anywhere), they began by preparing clear objectives, a work plan for the project, and performance expectations, which each member and senior management approved. It worked. The team met its time schedule, quality standards, cost objectives, and product reliability goals. Again, overarching mission and clear objectives drove the process.

Base Goals on a Defined Problem

The use of goals as a factor in creating a successful cross-functional team seems to work best when some development of the problem or issue has been done prior to the hand-off to the team. In the pharmaceutical industry, so-called discovery teams conduct preliminary research on the feasibility of a potential compound. If potential exists, the product is turned over to a cross-functional project team to carry the ball. In some telecommunications companies, a product line team identifies products to be developed and then turns over the promising ideas to a product development team for further development. In other industries, a senior management team or key leader develops ideas or identifies problems that are, in turn, handed off to a cross-functional team in the specific area. These teams then take the broad charter and turn it into a set of objectives and action plans. Taking the broad charter to the next level of specificity is critical to success because, as Barbara Bennett, vice president of human resources at The Stanley Works, points out in her response to our survey, "many teams have been slowed down by goals that were too broad."

Integrate Team Goals into Department Goals

Developing clear goals and an action plan only carries the process so far. It will only work if there are no problems or there is a senior management sponsor who is vitally interested in the project. These so-called high-profile projects will get whatever they want regardless of the process. However, for other teams, one more step helps make the goal-setting and implementation process work effectively. Team goals must be incorporated into the goals of each functional department and, where feasible, into the goals of each team member. In other words, both the department and the individual team member should have their contributions to the team effort included in the performance plan. This approach helps with the allocation of time and resources within the department and increases the likelihood that the team will get what it needs from the team member and the department. It also means that both the person and the department will be evaluated against those objectives, which, once again, will reinforce the importance of the cross-functional team's objectives. At Northern Telcom's facility in Research Triangle Park, North Carolina, Jim Kochanski, director of human resources, reports that the fact that "team goals are folded in with functional department goals is one of the critical success factors for our cross-functional teams" (interview with the author, January 1993).

WHY TEAMS
DON'T SET GOALS

One obvious question is, If we all agree that goal setting is important for the success of a cross-functional team, why don't more teams set effective goals? Here are some of the reasons we've encountered:

- We don't have time; we have a lot of work to do.
- This place is always in a state of crisis, so . . .
- We might look bad if we don't achieve the goals.
- Nobody looks at those things anyway.
- Nobody follows those things anyway.

- Our boss should set the goals; our job is to carry them out.
- The last person who did it isn't here anymore.

Take a look at your organization. What are some of the reasons your teams don't set effective goals? Make a list to get yourself to really think about it.

PLANNING
A TEAM'S FUTURE

A few definitions may help get your team started. Some people use these terms to mean the same thing, but each means something different and each serves a different purpose for a cross-functional team.

Vision

A vision is a statement of your preferred future. It's your hopes, dreams, and aspirations — or to put it another way, it's your druthers. It is what you *want* to achieve, not what you predict you actually will achieve. A vision may involve a significant change in a type of business, as when Federal Express pioneered the overnight delivery business; or it may involve an effort to regain market share, as when Xerox put customer satisfaction first and Ford made quality its number one concern. It is important for cross-functional team sponsors and team leaders that they not only have a vision but that they communicate it clearly and with enthusiasm. A vision is that broad umbrella that all team members can get under, regardless of their past experiences, prior commitments, or different team player styles.

Mission

A mission statement is a little closer to home. It communicates a team's fundamental purpose, its raison d'être. A mission (or charter, as it is sometimes called) states what you do and for whom you do it. To put it another way: A mission focuses on your function and your customers. It may also include your values or philosophy and your special talents or technology. For example, Cincinnati Milacron created a cross-functional team called Operation Wolfpack, whose mission was "to cut the fat from the organization, its processes, and its products, and to build in the agility to respond to market demands" (Johnson, 1992, p. 6). A mission statement should be brief and clear; it should also reflect the unique character, capability, or other features of the team. Most cross-functional teams shape their mission in response to a directive from upper management. This makes sense. Management should provide the team with a set of expectations and challenges. It is up to the team to give its own spin to the directive by creating a team charter.

Goals

With goal statements, teams begin to operationalize the planning process. Goals are statements of desired future states. They are long-term but possible outcomes. They should be based on the team's mission and vision. In those situations where the mission or vision has been handed to the team by senior management or some other group, the team then fashions the goals. Team goals are typically few in number, and although they have a target date (two to five years), they can be somewhat general. For example, a quality action team I worked with had the goal of "developing and implementing a program to provide each employee with an opportunity for individual recognition." A product development team set a goal of "reducing the time to market by 50 percent."

Objectives

The preparation of clear objectives is the key to a successful planning process. Without well-written objectives, the process will become simply a pie-in-the-sky effort that looks good only on paper. Objectives are short term (twelve months or less), specific, and usually, measurable outcome statements. The same quality action team mentioned in the previous section had as one of its project objectives to highlight the achievements of at least one employee in each issue of the department's newsletter. It's clear that the team's objectives become the rallying point for the team's current work, the vehicle for communicating with the functional departments, and the basis for setting priorities and allocating resources. Clearly, objectives are critical to the successful team-building of cross-functional teams. In a study of fifty teams in some thirty companies, two McKinsey and Company researchers found that "the best teams translate their common purposes into specific goals such as reducing the reject rate from suppliers by 50 percent or increasing the math scores of graduates from 40 to 95 percent" (Katzenbach and Smith, 1993a, p. 113).

Action Plans

Here is where the rubber meets the road. Each team objective must be translated into a series of tasks that when completed will result in the achievement of the objective. Action plans describe specific work assignments that are the responsibility of individual team members. Each step represents an activity that will be accomplished in one to twelve months. Taken together, all the steps constitute an action plan. I recommend an action plan format that simply lists the tasks to be performed, names the team member responsible for the task, and indicates the date the task is expected to be completed.

GOALS ARE NOT GLUE

All teams need goals. But cross-functional teams need them more. Since the cross-functional team brings together people from a variety of departments, each with his or her own goals, it is essential that the team develops a set of goals and performance objectives that all team members accept and support. Team goals become a focal point for these varied interests and a mechanism for setting priorities and resolving conflicts.

Consider these questions in assessing your team's common commitment:

1. Does your team have a clear purpose or mission? Is the mission based on a broader organizational mission or a challenge provided by upper management?

2. Is the team's mission a product of discussion and involvement by a broad range of team members?

3. Has the team's mission been translated into a specific set of performance objectives? Are the objectives clear, measurable, and specific? Do all members buy into these objectives?

4. Are all team members clear about their role in achieving these objectives? Do they feel accountable for their accomplishment?

5. Is there a work plan for achieving the objectives? Do members feel responsible for accomplishing the total plan, not just their part? Do members pitch in and help each other out?

A clear set of goals is critical to the success of a cross-functional team. Since the team is often composed of people with little experience in working together, goals can be the glue that holds this band of allies, enemies, and strangers together. However, goals by themselves cannot do the trick. A cross-functional team needs the help and support of others to achieve its goals. In the next chapter, I discuss how to effectively manage the boundaries with other key stakeholders in the organization.

C H A P T E R

7

Building Bridges
Outside the Team

To coin a phrase, No cross-functional team is an island. Although so much of the research and thinking about teams has focused on their internal dynamics, experts are only now coming to realize the importance of external relations, or what is sometimes called "managing the outside" (Hastings, Bixby, and Chaudhry-Lawton, 1987). The importance of building bridges for cross-functional teams should by now be obvious. Cross-functional teams are linked in many ways to many different people and organizations and in fact are dependent on others for their success. Some of these people may know your work and be supporters, some may have worked with you in the past and be potential barriers, and others may not be aware of your work and may need to be convinced of its value.

If the current proliferation of cross-functional teams is to be successful, there must be an emphasis on what is sometimes called *boundary management,* the process by which a team manages its "borders" and the flow of information and resources to and from its key stakeholders. The flow may be vertical (to senior management) or horizontal (to functional departments); and it is interactive, in the sense that the team both sends and receives information or resources to and from the stakeholders. A recent study of cross-functional new-product teams seems to indicate that effective boundary management can make a real difference: "high-performing product development teams carry out more external activity than low-performing teams. . . . High performers interacted more frequently with manufacturing, marketing, R&D, and top division management during all phases of activity. Members of high-performing teams did not simply react to communications from others; they were more likely to be the initiators of communication with outsiders than those individuals on low-performing teams" (Ancona and Caldwell, 1990b, p. 28).

As others have noted, cross-functional teams differ from functional teams in the way they emphasize effective boundary management. The unique nature of cross-functional teams makes it essential that they develop positive relationships with key stakeholders in the organization.

> The interdisciplinary work team differs from homogeneous groups in two major respects. First, it is an open rather than a closed system. A group's experience is often owed to some agent outside the group's boundaries who places requirements on the group in an unpredictable sequence. In performing its role, the group must import resources and export products across its boundaries to appropriate portions of the environment. In addition to the sociopsychological boundary that separates the group from its environment, other boundaries are more salient than in laboratory groups. Production schedules and commitments to outside agents emphasize temporal bounds [McCorcle, 1982, pp. 293–294].

McCorcle also points out that the cross-functional team must maintain an appropriate balance between external relations and internal team development. This drive toward interaction with the outside world coupled with the equally strong drive toward positive internal dynamics can provide the team with certain tension points. Properly managed, this tension can be helpful when it requires the team to look at two competing and important success factors.

THE KEY STAKEHOLDERS

Most cross-functional teams have the same kinds of important stakeholders although the number of stakeholders (and, of course, their names) will vary by organization. Therefore, each team must do its own stakeholder analysis and develop a plan to effectively manage the boundary.

Functional Department Managers

The department managers of the cross-functional team members are often in a make-or-break role in regard to the success of the team. They can freely give the resource—their employee—or they can keep the person on a tight leash. For the team to be successful, the functional department managers must

- Understand the purpose and priorities of the cross-functional team

- Allow and even encourage the team member to complete team assignments

- Clarify the team member's authority as the department's representative on the team and then allow the team member to exercise that authority

- Regularly communicate with the team member about the work of the team

- Periodically communicate with the team leader about the team's progress and the nature of the team member's work

- Obtain feedback from the team leader about the team member's performance

Customers and Clients

No team should exist without a customer or customers for its output; the customers may be internal or external to the organization and they may have varying levels of needs. The team's success depends on how well it interacts with its customers; it must continually obtain information from them about their needs and desires. Some teams designate specific team members as the client liaison, responsible for ongoing contact with the customer. Often this person is the project manager, but the client liaison can also be the product manager, client interface manager, or systems analyst. One of my clients, an automobile industry supplier, has designated customer representatives who are responsible for communication and plant visits with their automobile assembly customers.

Having a single point of contact is an efficient and often effective way of working with clients because it (1) makes it easier for clients to give feedback, (2) allows the team to designate, train, and develop one person skilled in client interface, and (3) eliminates the confusion that occurs when many team members talk to the same client. Some teams have reduced the stakeholder communication problem by having customers serve as members of the cross-functional team. The customers attend all meetings and provide their input throughout the process. (See Chapter Twelve for a discussion of customer participation on cross-functional teams.)

Senior Management

One of the key internal stakeholders is senior management, or more specifically, the senior manager who sponsored the cross-functional team. It is critical that the team keep management informed about the team's progress, successes, need for resources, potential problems (especially problems with clients), and changes in the timetable. Geri Weber, a leader and member of many cross-functional teams at Bell Communications Research, recommends that the team and particularly the team leader take responsibility for establishing a structure to ensure systematic feedback to management, even in those cases where no formal structure currently exists (interview with the author, January 1993).

Senior management does not like surprises, such as complaints from customers, delays in the project timetable, and unforeseen, last-minute problems. One cross-functional team in a major pharmaceutical company spent a great deal of time preparing a plan and developing internal communication processes but neglected to "sell" the concept sufficiently to senior management. Despite much good work and good intentions, the team and its concept were cancelled. In another company, a team prepared a careful market analysis of a potential product but the boss refused to fund the continuation of the project. Team members agreed that they had not brought him in early enough to gain his support.

In some situations, senior management is an ongoing member of the team. This can prove beneficial to the team. At Motorola's plant in Austin, Texas, a senior manager serves as team sponsor who helps the team get the resources it needs (Kumar and Gupta, 1991). In this case, resources can mean anything from an expert the team needs to help solve a problem to the procurement of a piece of equipment.

Support Groups and Service Departments

At various stages in its cycle, a cross-functional team needs assistance from other groups in the organization. The effective team builds and maintains positive relationships with these groups because their support is often in the form of tangible aid.

THE NEEDS OF CROSS-FUNCTIONAL TEAMS

Information

Ongoing empowered teams constantly need accurate and current information for daily decision making. Project teams, of various levels of empowerment, usually have a great need for information at the outset of a project. They need customer and market data about the potential need for the product, system, or service. Quality action teams need data about the nature and extent of the problem. All cross-functional teams have to draw data from the political winds in the organization to see if there is support for the team's project.

Resources

At some point, the team will need some "stuff." The types of resources that teams often need from support and service groups include:

- *People* — from experts to offer advice and do real work to extra hands to pitch in and get the work done

- *Product* — from the production of a prototype to the supply of test samples for a field trial

- *Research* — from statistical studies or laboratory experiments to focus groups or field tests

Support

Something of an intangible, support groups can truly support the team by helping the team get what it needs. They can do this in an easy, no-hassle manner and in a professional and timely fashion. On the other hand, if the team has to fight to get the support it needs, to get the work done quickly, to get it done correctly, then the whole process breaks down.

Awareness of Impact

Cross-functional teams need to be aware of the impact of their work on other groups in the organization. For example, a team may come up with a wonderful new procedure that reduces the time it takes to get the job done—but this new procedure may cause problems for another group. At one plant, the team on the C shift came up with a way to speed up their work by eliminating set-up for the next job; their time improved but the A shift was left with extra work. Effective teamwork requires collaboration among teams.

BARRIERS TO BRIDGE BUILDING

Despite all the good reasons for effective interteam relationships, groups in organizations often do not work well together. Cross-functional teams do not manage their boundaries well, do not get the support they need, do not get the resources they require, and fail as a result. Before looking at methods for achieving positive external relations, let's look at the causes of breakdowns in the process.

Stereotyping

Yes, plain old-fashioned prejudice. Team members come to a relationship with preconceived ideas about how certain groups behave. These stereotypes stand in the way of building positive relationship bridges. Think about the stakeholder groups we identified—how are they perceived by cross-functional teams in your organization? Exhibit 7.1 gives examples of some typical stereotypes about these stakeholders. Feel free to add some perceptions of your own.

Competition

Groups in organizations are in competition. There is nothing wrong with some healthy competition between teams in an

Exhibit 7.1. Stereotypes About Stakeholders.

---

1. *Senior Management.* "All they care about is the bottom line." "They don't know what it's like out here in the real world." "When's the last time they talked to a real customer?"
Add Your Own:

2. *Functional Department Managers.* "All they care about is meeting their personal objectives." "They see this cross-functional teamwork stuff as an annoyance." "For them, the cross-functional team is something they give to but get nothing back in return."
Add Your Own:

3. *Customers and Clients.* "All they want is more for less." "They never tell us their needs upfront but sure do have a lot of comments on the finished product."
Add Your Own:

4. *Support Groups.* "Ask those market research people for some help and they dump a stack of useless data on you." "You know how those lawyers are, they'll find all the reasons why you shouldn't do it." "Ever try getting a *fast* answer out of an engineer?"
Add Your Own:

5. *Other Internal Units.* "All they care about is making it easier for themselves." "They never did anything for us, why should we do anything to help them?"
Add Your Own:

organization; competition to be the best team, to get to the market faster, to solve a complex problem, to bring in the most sales are all examples of positive competitive goals. But if a team tries to achieve a goal at another's expense, for example, by not sharing resources or information, it is negative competition. Unhealthy competition can stand in the way of healthy collaboration, which is a key to successful cross-functional teamwork.

Teams compete for all sorts of things:

- Recognition for their efforts
- Budget to continue or expand their project
- Tangible rewards and compensation
- Opportunities to work on high-visibility, interesting projects
- Use of internal resources

Differentiation

Depending upon the degree of certainty in the environment, groups in an organization need to be differentiated (Lawrence and Lorsch, 1967). As groups become more differentiated in their work styles, practices, and orientations, the challenge of integrating them increases. Although this differentiation helps units in an organization pull together to get the work done, it can be a barrier when they have to work collaboratively with a cross-functional team. Tension ensues because the need to maintain differentiation is at odds with the need to integrate effort.

STRATEGIES FOR
BRIDGE BUILDING

Cross-functional teams need to recognize the importance of managing the outside. Beyond this recognition is the necessity of taking action—planning to work effectively with the key stakeholders. Certain actions can help.

Identify the Key Stakeholders

Begin by making a list of the people and groups you need to ensure your team's success. Include the things you need from these stakeholders. Make up another list of people and groups who have something to gain and something to lose from the work of your team. For example, if you come up with some cost-saving ideas or quality improvements, will some people stand to lose their jobs as a result?

Look for Commonalities

Look beyond what you need from the identified stakeholders to see what you can do for them. In what ways do they need your ideas, your help, or other things they might get from you? The net result of this analysis should be a set of *common* objectives—outcomes you both share. Is there an umbrella you can both get under?

Communicate Information

Find ways to tell others about your team. Use reports, meeting minutes, newsletters, company publications, and other written methods to communicate with your key stakeholders. But in most cases, verbal communication still works best. Look for opportunities to make formal presentations as well as have informal chats (at lunch, in the hallways, at the copy machine, and other places where you can report to groups of managers, customers, and others in the organization). For example, each team member representing a functional department should have the ongoing responsibility of keeping his or her manager informed and "sold" on the team's project. Some teams also ask key stakeholders to come to team meetings to hear firsthand how the team is doing.

Select Boundary Managers

The best cross-functional teams carefully select the team members who will handle the key interfaces. They do not assume that the team leader will do all of this work. They ask, What needs to be done and who is the best person to do it? We need some help from the people in the computer center — who has worked successfully with them in the past? We need to get budget approval for some additional field studies, let's ask Arlene to talk with them because she used to work over there. One of our customers has a complaint about the product, why not ask Ming to handle it, since she helped develop the prototype?

Identify Potential Barriers

An important aspect of building relationships with key stakeholders is looking at potential barriers. For example, ask,

- Are there any past problems that need to be resolved or overcome?

- Are you in competition with this group?

- Does this group stand to lose as a result of your team's project?

- Does this group support the concept of cross-functional teamwork?

- Do you respect this group?

Once the team has identified the actual barriers, it can prepare a plan for overcoming them and achieving successful relationships with stakeholders.

Be Credible

All these strategies work only if you and your team members are credible, only if other people can depend on you and your word. Assess yourself and your team. Do other people trust you? Can they count on you . . . to deliver on promises . . . to tell the truth? In developing positive relationships with key stakeholders,

- Don't ask for more than you need.
- Don't promise more than you plan to deliver.
- Don't set a due date you can't possibly meet.
- Don't exaggerate project benefits or results.

Prepare an Analysis and a Plan

You can use Exhibit 7.2 as a planning tool for building bridges to key stakeholders for your cross-functional team. If you identify several stakeholders, divide the task by asking individual members or groups of members to each do an analysis of one of the stakeholders.

Once you have completed a thorough analysis of your key stakeholders and have a plan for building positive relationships, move on to the next chapter, where the focus is on a subject of vital importance to every team member — performance appraisal. All your good work in developing clear goals and boundary management can come apart if team members do not feel that their work on the cross-functional team is valued and incorporated into their regular performance appraisal.

Exhibit 7.2.   Building Bridges Worksheet.

---

1. Identify a person, department, or other team that your team needs in order to be successful.

2. What *specific* types of help do you need from this stakeholder?

3. What kinds of assistance or input does the stakeholder need from your team?

4. Identify common objectives you share with the stakeholder.

5. What potential barriers may prevent the stakeholder and your team from working together effectively?

6. How can you overcome these barriers?

7. Which member of your team would be the best person to work with the stakeholder?

8. What specific steps can you take to develop a positive relationship with the stakeholder?

C H A P T E R

8

Appraising Teamwork and Team Members

Why should I knock myself out doing work for this team
when none of what I do here gets included in my
annual performance appraisal?
—Question asked by many cross-functional team members

Why should I knock myself out trying to be a
good team player when all that
really counts around here is your individual contribution?
—Question asked by many cross-functional team members

Cross-functional team members can go only so far on the strength of charisma and calls for commitment. Eventually, team members are going to ask how they personally will benefit from their participation on the team. In fact, most people's favorite station is WIFM—What's in It for Me. Performance appraisal is one of the most important avenues for obtaining credit for work on a cross-functional team, and appraisals often result in salary increases, promotions, or new assignments.

PERFORMANCE APPRAISAL AND TEAMWORK: IRRECONCILABLE DIFFERENCES?

Deming seems to think so (Deming, 1987). Deming's famous fourteen points for achieving continuous quality improvement include the elimination of the annual employee evaluation process because it diminishes or destroys the importance of teamwork. The traditional and, up to now, typical performance appraisal focuses on individual performance as assessed by the employee's supervisor. In this process, the emphasis is on technical excellence, assignments completed, objectives reached, and individual productivity. Even when general factors such as cooperation and teamwork are included, the assessment is still based only on the supervisor's view of his or her immediate team. Performance on cross-functional teams is rarely considered.

The problem intensifies when the appraisal process is combined with a competitive rating system. In this system, a pool of money is budgeted for raises and is distributed based on the ranking of all employees in a unit. Although employees are usually not told their ranking, they know they are in competition with their colleagues in the ranking process. The result is that people are more likely to be competitive than collaborative with their teammates. I have interviewed employees in companies with this system who will say flat out, "Why should I help my officemates or teach them something I know when, at the end of the year, we'll be competing with each other in the ranking process for a bigger share of the pie?" Even when team members want to be collaborative, the system does not allow it: "Two employees who had to work together throughout the year and enjoyed being team players tried an experiment. During the year, all of their work (reports, programs, and memos) was published under joint authorship. They accomplished a great deal and were satisfied with their effort as a team. However, in preparation for the annual division appraisal meeting, their manager asked that they indicate specifically who prepared each document. The system required that there be some way of differentiating them!" (Parker, 1990, p. 146).

The situation is exaggerated when employees spend a great deal of their time serving on cross-functional teams. If their supervisor is solely responsible for their appraisal, he or she usually does not have a clear view of their work and is often unable to include an assessment of their performance on these teams in the total appraisal. And if teamwork is not a valued behavior in the organization, then the supervisor is not likely to make the effort to include teamwork in the appraisal.

All these factors tend to have a very negative impact on the success of cross-functional teams. I have talked with many cross-functional team members who are unhappy with the situation because they believe all their efforts on behalf of the team are not considered in their appraisal. Other team members interviewed simply make tactical choices between their functional department work and their cross-functional team assignments. Clearly, when there is any doubt, they choose to complete their department assignments first. Team leaders are frustrated by this situation also, because it limits their ability to get their project completed.

PRESSURES ON PERFORMANCE APPRAISAL

Fortunately, not all is lost. The performance appraisal process is beginning to change in response to pressures in the work environment. These changes will have a positive effect on cross-functional teams.

Emphasis on Teams as a Business Strategy

As organizations make greater and greater use of cross-functional and self-directed teams, there will be increased pressure to include feedback from team leaders and team members in the appraisal process. Increasingly, supervisors will not have a clear view of a great deal of the work of their subordinates. Therefore, they must get input from cross-functional team leaders.

Quality Initiatives

Most serious quality efforts are team based. As companies search for factors that will support their quality teams, they are seeing the importance of including teamwork in the appraisal process.

Downsizing

The flattening of organizations in the last ten years has resulted in a reduction in the number of supervisors, which has naturally increased the responsibilities of the remaining supervisors. Because they have so many employees to supervise, they can't possibly see everyone's work; as a result, they have to rely on the input of others, including peers, team leaders, and other supervisors.

Credibility

Employees are less and less satisfied with the performance feedback they receive from their supervisors. At one company, for example, less than 50 percent of the employees agreed with the statement, My immediate supervisor provides feedback about my performance that is helpful to me in performing my job. As a consequence, performance feedback as a motivator of employees is less effective. Employees are more responsive to feedback from colleagues, team leaders, and customers, who they believe have a more accurate perception of their performance.

Cultural Diversity

As the work force of America changes dramatically to include increasing numbers of employees from a wide variety of cultural groups, the pressures to more accurately assess their performance increase. The traditional white male supervisor is often less able to understand the behavior of women employees and employees of Asian, African, or Latin American descent. For these employees, obtaining feedback from multiple sources is on the rise. "Studies show compelling evidence that multirater systems yield, for example, higher performance measures for women than do traditional supervisor-only measures" (Edwards, 1991, p. 96).

CHANGES IN THE APPRAISAL PROCESS

All the pressures discussed above have resulted in some changes in the performance appraisal process and specifically in its application to cross-functional teams.

Changing Performance Criteria

Performance criteria are changing to incorporate teamwork behaviors in employee evaluations. Phrases such as "shares information with others," "negotiates differences effectively," "encourages and acknowledges the contributions of others," and "encourages cooperation and teamwork among people in his or her group and people in other groups in the company" are increasingly showing up on appraisal forms. The net effect is to send a message to employees that performance as a team member and team leader will be considered in the overall appraisal. Yes, we are still looking at individual performance but we are now considering how well the individual works in the team context. It's working. I am aware of certain technically talented individuals at one company who received lower ratings because they were perceived to be uncooperative team players. At another company, Bull HN Information Systems (the North American arm of France's Groupe Bull), David Dotlich says that "your ability to work in teams, to get things done through people, and to build teams, is a critical criterion around which we are now ranking people" (McClenahen, 1990, p. 23).

Incorporating Team Participation

Companies are no longer relying on the single supervisory evaluation for an assessment of employees' performance on teams. Increasingly, supervisors are asking team leaders for data on the performance of their employees who spend considerable time on cross-functional teams. At Hewlett-Packard, Stuart Winby reports that "you [project managers] get E-mail from functional managers all the time asking for input on people who are on your teams. They know they can't write an effective evaluation without going to team leaders, customers, and others who have a more objective view of how the employee works in a team setting" (interview with the author, February 1993). Hewlett-Packard has no formal procedure that requires including these data; it is just done because it makes sense. Even an informal approach can have the desired effect on employee behavior when it becomes a visible part of the culture. For example, at Intel's plant in Hillsboro, Oregon, "the managers of all departments regularly exchange information about how well their subordinates have served on project teams. That tends to keep everyone on their toes, . . . ready to do the extras like coming in early to call the East Coast for information" (Dowst and Raia, 1988, p. 85).

International Flavors and Fragrances (IFF), a company that consistently ranks at the top of the Fortune list of America's Most Admired Corporations, quickly found that in order to solidify its quality effort, team members had to get "credit" for their participation. IFF's Michael D'Aromando reports that participation on cross-functional quality teams is included in the performance appraisal form, and as a result, "people know we are serious" (interview with the author, February 1993). D'Aromando says that supervisors find out about the performance of their employees on teams by (1) chatting informally with team leaders, (2) getting feedback from facilitators, and (3) occasionally sitting in on meetings.

Keeping It Informal

Members of cross-functional teams that are in the coordinating and semiempowered stages will continue to be appraised by their functional managers with input provided by team leaders and other key team stakeholders. At the moment, most organizations are struggling to develop a process that incorporates performance data from people who have important information to share with the functional manager about the team member. Thus far, a simple informal process seems to have worked best. The functional manager simply asks for feedback on the person and the information is included in the overall assessment. In some cases, team leaders will actually fill out the company appraisal form as if a person were their official subordinate. As Bill Hines of Bell Communications Research (Bellcore) points out, "I follow the basic approach of our PMP [Performance Management Program] for each of these people" (interview with the author, January 1993). However, Bellcore has no formal policy that requires a manager to complete a PMP form; it just seems like a good idea to some managers because it means that they've considered all the important factors.

In some cases, performance feedback for participation on cross-functional teams is part of the formal evaluation process. For example, at the Robert Wood Johnson Pharmaceutical Research Institute (a Johnson and Johnson company), team leaders and members are evaluated on an annual basis with a link to a compensation bonus (as a response to my survey indicated).

Team Appraisals

As cross-functional teams move to the empowered stage, the opportunity for team member appraisals conducted by other team members increases. Studies of self-directed teams have shown that as a team becomes fully functioning and empowered, it takes on such former management responsibilities as hiring, firing, discipline, performance appraisal, and compensation (Wellins, Byham, and Wilson, 1991). There have been some earlier experiments with team appraisals.

At the Digital Equipment Corporation (DEC) plant in Colorado Springs, Colorado, self-directed teams are using a team appraisal process that is quite comprehensive. Each team member receives input from every other team member and works with a five-person committee that coordinates the appraisal process. The member selects the committee chairperson, who in turn selects the other committee members.

> The five committee members are: the individual whose PA [performance appraisal] is due; the chairperson; the management consultant; and two other co-workers in the group, randomly selected from a list of team members kept by the secretary. As soon as possible, the evaluee sends mail to the team members. . . outlining his or her accomplishments and training for the past year. This information is used as a base for the team to provide input, which must be done within two weeks. The input is then collected by the chairperson and a copy is sent to the individual being evaluated.
>
> The subject writes his or her own PA document from the input received by the chairperson. Then he or she sends a copy of the PA document to the committee for their review. The document and all input are reviewed, which takes one week, and the committee and the evaluee meet. If the PA needs further revision or additional input, another rating is determined based on the input, and the committee jointly sets the goals for the next year.
>
> Finally, the chairperson writes a summary of the meeting, including the rating and any promotion (if applicable). The completed document is printed and signed by the committee, subject and the management consultant. It's then submitted to the personnel department. Within two weeks, the committee and the evaluee formulate a development and job plan for the coming year [Norman and Zawacki, 1991, pp. 101–102].

Procter & Gamble is also tossing out the old supervisor-as-God performance appraisal process as the company makes the transition to a culture dotted with many cross-functional teams. Much like the DEC procedure described above, the person being assessed sits down with his or her boss to select a group of people who can provide input on the person's performance. "The appraisers receive detailed surveys that ask them to answer open-ended questions about the employee's performance: What does the candidate do well? What could be improved? This unique database is consolidated and used as the centerpiece of the formal performance appraisal discussion" (Austin, 1992, pp. 32, 34).

In much the same way, Eastman Chemical, a subsidiary of Eastman Kodak, is moving toward a total team-based organization. In the process, it is creating a team appraisal system that puts a different spin on the peer review concept operating at DEC and Procter & Gamble. It is reminiscent of the old sensitivity exercise, Hot Spot, where each member of the group takes a turn receiving feedback from everyone else. At Eastman Chemical, team member appraisals are conducted at a team meeting. Each team member in turn goes to the flip chart, where he or she writes a list of personal strengths and weaknesses. Other team members add to the list in the course of an open discussion. The company reports that this is not easy to pull off. The process requires lots of trust and collaboration, and management is providing the teams with training in these areas (Austin, 1992).

Perhaps sensing a potential growth market here, a consultant has stepped in and created a computer-based team appraisal process. The system incorporates survey feedback data from a supervisor and four colleagues. This multirater system, called the Team Evaluation and Management System (TEAMS), was developed by Dr. Mark R. Edwards, director of the Laboratory for Innovation and Decision Research at Arizona State University in Tempe, Arizona (Edwards, 1989).

Although still in the minority, team appraisal systems are increasing in number as organizations make greater use of teams, especially cross-functional and self-directed teams. In the meantime, those organizations that do not use the team appraisal systems must align the performance appraisal system with the new emphasis on cross-functional teams. The factors used to assess performance must reflect team player characteristics and the process must ensure that observed performance on teams is included in the appraisal.

TEAM PLAYER STYLES

In a previous study, I set out to identify the characteristics of an effective team player (Parker, 1990). The initial purpose of the study was to help a client organization change its performance appraisal process to reflect its vision of becoming a team-based culture. The leadership of the organization wanted to align the factors on the assessment form with the company's emphasis on teamwork as a key strategy. In the end, I found that there were four types of team players, each with a unique set of strengths. I called these team player styles Contributor, Collaborator, Communicator, and Challenger and developed a list of behaviors associated with each style. Many organizations have used these lists to incorporate specific team player behaviors in their performance appraisal form.

Contributor

1. Freely shares all relevant information and opinions with other team members.
2. Helps the team use its time and resources.
3. Pushes the team to set high standards and to achieve top-level results; insists on high-quality standards.
4. Completes all team assignments and other relevant homework necessary for the completion of team tasks.
5. Accepts responsibility for all actions as a team member.
6. Completes all work in his or her regular area and in other tasks not related to the team.
7. Provides the team with clear, concise, and useful presentations at team meetings.

8. Provides technical training for other team members and serves as a mentor for new team members.

9. Has a clear set of priorities.

Collaborator

1. Helps the team establish long-term goals and clarify its current objective or task.

2. Helps the team see how its work fits into the total organization.

3. Regularly reminds the team of the need to revisit the goals and action plans.

4. Encourages the team to establish plans with milestones and appropriate task assignments.

5. Pitches in to help out other team members who need assistance.

6. Works hard to achieve team goals and to complete the current tasks, even though he or she may not agree with them.

7. Does not gossip about other team members or share negative comments about team process with nonmembers.

8. Is flexible and open to new ideas or data that may alter team goals.

9. Often works outside his or her defined role to help the team achieve its goals.

10. Is willing to share the limelight with other team members.

Communicator

1. Steps in to resolve process problems, such as conflict among team members or lack of involvement by some team members.

2. Listens attentively to all viewpoints while withholding judgment.

3. Helps the team relax and have fun by joking, laughing, and discussing personal interests.

4. Recognizes and praises other team members for their efforts.

5. Communicates enthusiasm and a sense of urgency about the team's work.

6. Periodically summarizes the status of a discussion or proposes a possible consensus.

7. Encourages other team members to participate in the discussions and decisions on the team.

8. Helps the people on the team get to know each other and to know what skills and resources each can contribute.

9. Gives feedback to other team members that is descriptive, specific, and intended to be helpful.

10. Receives feedback from other team members without becoming defensive.

11. Reminds the team to take the time periodically to assess team effectiveness and plan for improvement.

Challenger

1. Candidly shares views about the work of the team.

2. Is willing to disagree openly with the leadership of the team.

3. Often raises questions about the team's goals.

4. Pushes the team to set high ethical standards for work.

5. Speaks out even when views are contrary to those of a vast majority of the team.

6. Asks *why* and *how* and other relevant questions at team meetings.

7. Sometimes is accused of not being a team player because he or she differs with the conventional wisdom.

8. Challenges the team to take well-conceived risks.

9. Is honest in reporting team progress and stating problems facing the team.

10. Is willing to blow the whistle on illegal and unethical activities of the team.

11. Will back off when views are not accepted and will support a legitimate team consensus.

TECHNIQUES FOR APPRAISING PERFORMANCE ON CROSS-FUNCTIONAL TEAMS

While not the result of a research study, my observation from numerous conversations with cross-functional team members is that performance appraisal is a critical factor for success. Team members want to be sure that their performance on cross-functional teams is included in their appraisal. It affects their performance because it is linked to their motivation. Fortunately, it is not terribly complicated to alter the performance appraisal process to include assessment of cross-functional teams.

Incorporate Team Participation in the Appraisal

Whether formal or informal, you have simply got to make sure that the managers responsible for employee appraisals reach out to cross-functional team leaders for their input on team members. I recently worked with a department manager who told me that all her people worked on cross-functional teams. She managed a group of technical experts whose primary job was to serve as resources to a variety of teams. In fact, she rarely saw them. The only way she could prepare a fair evaluation of their performance was to obtain feedback from project team leaders.

Include Team Player Behaviors in the Appraisal

If we believe that performance on cross-functional teams should be included in the appraisal process, then we must revise the appraisal form to include specific behaviors associated with the success of these teams. Earlier in this chapter, I described four types of team player behaviors that can be used as a basis for revising the performance appraisal form. In Chapter Twelve you will find a description of the characteristics of team members required for effective participation on cross-functional teams.

The appraisal process in most organizations sets the foundation for decisions about compensation. Appraisal and compensation are important because we want effective team players to be rewarded with added salary. However, our research indicates that salary treatment is necessary but not sufficient for the development of a team-based organization. An effective rewards and recognition program must be part of the package. In the next chapter, a variety of options are presented, followed by some specific conclusions about the design of a positive rewards system.

C H A P T E R

9

Team Pay
for Team Play

The drive for teamwork in organizations, especially cross-functional teamwork, is way ahead of the systems needed to support the change. Although training and technology systems are moving fast to support the rapid expansion of cross-functional teamwork, performance appraisal, compensation, and rewards are lagging behind. This situation needs to change fast. As I have said, charismatic leadership and calls for commitment will carry an organization only so far. Eventually, and it's happening already in many organizations I know, teams and team players will want to be rewarded for doing the right thing. This whole movement to team-based organizations, including total quality efforts, will be derailed unless we find ways to reward people for their team efforts. We are still a long way from widespread use of processes that reward teamwork. A Wilson Learning Corporation study of 4,500 teams in more than 500 organizations found that in 80 percent of the

117

organizations the rewards and compensation systems still focused on individual behavior ("Organizational, Individual Factors Pose Biggest Barriers for Teams").

The pressure to develop creative responses to the growth of teamwork is resulting in more group incentive plans in organizations. A Towers-Perrin study of group incentive plans among Fortune 1000 firms found that the number of plans was still quite small; however, one-half of the plans had been in operation for less than three years, indicating that their use is on the rise (Kanin-Lovers, 1990). Organizations interested in supporting cross-functional teams can study the team reward systems that have been around for some time, such as gain-sharing, suggestion systems, and skill- or knowledge-based pay. Until recently, most of these programs operated primarily in manufacturing settings and in a few front-line service departments. We need to see if these programs can work in other service areas as well as among knowledge workers, where there is a proliferation of cross-functional teamwork.

REWARDING TEAMWORK

Old Wine, Old Bottle

Gainsharing.   The relatively new term *gainsharing* is growing in popularity, as organizations look for ways to respond to the pressure to reward teamwork. I first heard this term about ten years ago at a conference, but it describes a group of reward programs that have been around since the 1930s. The oldest and still the best known of these approaches is the Scanlon Plan. Other programs are the Rucker Plan and Improshare. One might also include profit sharing in this category, although rarely is it used as an incentive to encourage teamwork, except to the degree that a companywide measure can do the job.

My purpose here is not to provide a detailed explanation of the inner workings of gainsharing plans but to review the landscape of possibilities for organizations looking for programs of financial incentives that encourage cross-functional teamwork. A great deal has been written about gainsharing and its results (McAdams and Hawk, 1992; Lawler, 1988; O'Dell and McAdams, 1987). The goal of the program is to "share the gains" of the efforts of employees with those same employees. All the variations have financial formulas for measuring performance (usually labor costs) improvements in productivity and then sharing the gains in the form of cash payments or noncash awards (merchandise and travel). From the standpoint of our interest in rewarding successful cross-functional teamwork, it is important to note that rewards are distributed to employees on the basis of the performance of their team. However, the plans differ in the definition of the unit designated as a team — it can vary from a small work group to the entire organization. Obviously, the larger the unit and the farther away the unit is from actual work teams in the organization, the lesser the impact on team performance.

It should be noted that most gainsharing plans have an employee involvement component, such as a suggestion system or quality circles. In fact, Lawler (1986) says that "in most cases, a participative system is needed in order for gainsharing to work; and in virtually every case, it is needed in order for the potential of the plan to be realized" (p. 152). However, it is very important to understand that in most of these plans there is no *direct* relationship between employee suggestions, team recommendations, other team efforts, and the payoffs from the program. It is *assumed* that the sum total of all of these team activities will be reflected in the overall cost savings and ultimately in the awards.

While most studies of gainsharing programs indicate that the programs achieve their objectives, there are some problems with their application to the cross-functional team concept:

1. How do you measure cost savings or productivity gains in service and knowledge teams?

2.   In large organizations, how do you make the *line-of-sight* connection between the performance of the team and the reward; that is, how do you get team members to see the relationship between their performance and the reward?

3.   How do you reward the people who provide the necessary support and service to the team?

Despite these problems, it is also important to recognize the key concept of all gainsharing programs: Rewards are directly related to performance. In other words, if the team succeeds, team members will be rewarded. We must keep this in mind as we look for ways to reward cross-functional teamwork.

Knowledge-Based Pay.   Sometimes known as skill-based pay, this system has already been applied to cross-functional teams where cross-training of team members is critical to team success. Team members are encouraged to learn new skills and receive pay increments when they can demonstrate that the skills have been acquired. For example, "At Johnsonville Foods in Sheboygan Falls, Wisconsin, the 600-member work force is divided into 14 cross-functional teams. Employees receive a base pay according to the market value of their jobs. When a team member believes she's ready to advance within her salary range, she asks her peers to review her performance. They decide where she has mastered a series of skills called 'result blocks.' If the answer is yes, she gets the raise" (Sisco, 1992, p. 43). Johnsonville is also working on bonus systems that provide payoffs to teams that exceed goals and individuals who (1) exceed quality and efficiency standards and (2) teach their teammates something new. In this way, the company supports the team learning concept while recognizing outstanding individual performance.

The knowledge-based pay program at the Aid Association for Lutherans (AAL) insurance company is a good example of how this reward system is used to foster more effective cross-functional teamwork in the service sector. Cross-training of team members has dramatically improved the quality of service to the company's field agents. All members of the team are able to handle any request that comes in from the field. Much like the Johnsonville plan, team members receive pay increments as they acquire and *use* new skills.

Another insurance company that has successfully used knowledge-based pay is Shenandoah Life Insurance Company in Roanoke, Virginia. "Shenandoah now assigns teams of 5 to 15 people to serve all the agents and life insurance accounts in a geographical region. Team members must each perform 17 jobs that in the past were separate including processing applications for policies, rating risks, computing premiums, checking data, and maintaining accounts receivable. For each job that they learn and are able to perform, team members get a raise. The results: pay for the 75 employees on teams has increased an average of 37.6 percent in the last two years, while the rest of Shenandoah Life employees have received average increases of 5 percent" (O'Dell, 1989, pp. 41–42).

The payoff for Shenandoah has been significant. Volume of work has increased 33 percent while costs have been reduced by two hundred thousand dollars. Although fewer people are now needed in this operation, no one has been laid off; people have been transferred to other parts of the business.

Knowledge-based pay rewards the behavior of cross-functional team members. It assumes that these behaviors will have a direct impact on the success of the team and the overall success of the company. It works in those team situations where cross-team learning is critical to the team's success, but the system does not require that team results take place before team members receive their reward. Demonstrating and using the behaviors on the job is sufficient. One of the key benefits of knowledge-based pay as a motivator is that it clearly meets the line-of-sight criterion for team reward programs. In other words, it is very easy for team members to see the relationship between their performance and the payoff.

Thus far, the discussion has focused on what might be called horizontal skill building; that is, learning the skills and acquiring the knowledge of other team members' jobs. This type of training reduces downtime in production operations, improves customer service, encourages collaboration among team members, and facilitates process improvement. Because team members are able to perform many tasks, they can see how the total process works and how it can be improved. It is here that the company may begin to realize quality and cost benefits, especially when there is a strong employee participation component to the process.

Although much less recognized, vertical skill building is another way for team members to improve performance: Employees could upgrade their skills in the same function. A software developer can learn a new programming language, a marketing specialist can learn to use more complex market analysis tools, or an electrician can learn how to fix a new piece of automated equipment. Employees who improve their skills vertically are able to make more in-depth contributions to the team. The technical specialty they bring to the team is now more valuable and the team is stronger, therefore knowledge-based pay systems can reward this type of behavior. However, it must be clear that the added knowledge will indeed add value to the team.

Clearly, some cross-functional teams are already using knowledge-based pay with success, primarily in production operations and in some front-line service functions. The question is, Can it be expanded to other cross-functional teams, such as product or systems development teams, process re-engineering teams, quality action teams, or teams that include high-level professionals who come together on a project basis? The answer lies in the perceived need for cross-team learning. In other words, Would the team benefit from team members learning more about the work of the other functions represented on the team? The answers vary. For a basic coordinating team, where members simply contribute pieces to a plan, the answer is probably no. But for a semiempowered project team that may exist for an extended period of time, team members might find it very useful to be able to understand and use the tools of other disciplines.

One important benefit would be the ability to ask questions about work done in another field. Certainly as organizations move to the creation of permanent cross-functional professional teams, this need will increase. As I have indicated, some consulting firms have already established ongoing multidisciplinary teams that focus on major clients or market segments. In such teams, it is extremely valuable for team members to build skills both vertically and horizontally. Team members should be rewarded for the acquisition of new knowledge, just as teachers are rewarded with automatic pay increases as they complete advanced degree and certificate programs.

We need to remember that much of the team learning described in Chapter Ten is informal and self-directed. Professional and technical team members often expand their knowledge base as a result of their participation on cross-functional teams. We need to find ways to include this type of learning in schemes to reward team members for their additional knowledge and skills. As Michael White, a compensation expert with Towers Perrin, has concluded:

> The growing use of cross-functional project teams...
> contributes to the need for more innovative approaches
> to the reward system. These teams bring individuals to-
> gether on a project basis from various functions...to
> work on new products or services or solve specific prob-
> lems. Because they've worked so closely with the other
> team members, these individuals generally return to their
> units with broadened skills and knowledge that must be
> recognized, nurtured, and rewarded. In addition, the flex-
> ibility of the team structure means that an individual
> might be a leader of one team and a participant on
> another, calling for a fluid approach to compensation that
> reinforces continuous skill development and enhance-
> ment [White, 1991, p. 15].

Old Wine, New Bottle

Some organizations are experimenting with more direct payments to teams for specific results. These so-called bonus or team incentive plans vary in format. If there is a continuum for team rewards, incentive programs fall somewhere between individual rewards for participation on teams and gainsharing or profit-sharing programs. Bonus plans tend to be tailored to the type of work done by the team or to a specific organizational goal such as reduced costs or time to market, or quality improvement. Not all programs provide cash awards; many reward team members with merchandise or services that have substantial value.

One-Time Bonuses.   Temporary teams that come together for a specific purpose and for a defined period of time (usually a short time) can be offered a team bonus for achieving various objectives. Objectives such as on-time, ahead-of-schedule, or under-budget delivery or cost-saving ideas can be clearly spelled out and tied directly to team awards. For example, in 1987 Honeywell's Space Systems Group had a chance to win a major contract with the Air Force for highly specialized computer chips, if the group could design the best chip first (O'Dell, 1989). The objective was to turn out perfect chips and cut down the design time. Honeywell's project manager came up with what might be called a bounty system. He offered to pay each engineer $150 when a chip passed the first design step on target and up to $1,200 when three chips passed in one design cycle; the team could receive up to $4,000 for similar passes. It worked. The team designed two chips perfectly in the first cycle, which put Honeywell some nine months ahead of IBM, its nearest competitor.

General Electric also used a bonus plan to motivate a cross-functional team of engineers, technicians, and plant layout specialists responsible for the start-up of a new plant in Mexico. There were three milestones for each phase of the plant's development plus a quality milestone linked to the failure of any new product during the initial warranty period after the plant began production.

Cost Reduction and Revenue Enhancement Programs.
Doherty, Nord, and McAdams (1989) have provided us with a

useful distinction between types of plans: performance improvement programs (PIPs) and team suggestion programs (TSPs). A PIP provides rewards for actual improvement in performance while a TSP pays for suggestions that reduce costs or increase revenues. Both programs focus on the efforts of individual teams and offer noncash awards in the form of merchandise. The TSP awards are based on the estimated value of the suggestion — that is, how much money the idea will save the company. Both programs can be temporary; PIPs run for less than two years while TSPs run for several months. Within the past few years, however, more companies are using PIPs and TSPs as ongoing plans, with adjustments in plan design to reflect changing business objectives. An example is American Airlines, which started its AAdvantage plans as a ninety-day TSP. The first TSP was so successful, with savings of over $60 million in the first year, that the plans are now in their fifth year, with increased savings every year.

PIPs establish objectives for improvement in areas such as productivity, quality, safety, and absenteeism. Baseline figures for a previous period are established and rewards are given for results that exceed the baseline. Awards in the form of vouchers are distributed monthly or quarterly, based on the team's actual improvements against the baseline. The return on investment (cost of awards) averages 3:1 or 200 percent, with a payout of 2 to 3 percent of base pay per employee per year (McAdams and Hawk, 1992).

TSPs are short-term programs designed to increase revenues or reduce costs using a team-based suggestion system. Teams are given one hour per week to generate ideas, calculate the dollar amount of the savings or revenue increase, and prepare a proposal. A management review committee evaluates the proposal and decides on its merits. If a proposal is accepted and it will save at least five hundred dollars, each team member receives award points based on the first-year net savings or revenues.

Team Incentive Systems. Some organizations are experimenting with less complicated incentive programs for teams.

Once again, these programs are attempts to bring the awards down to the team level, in an effort to improve the line of sight between team performance and the payoff. In a very interesting effort with a team of knowledge workers, a biotechnology company has developed a program that provides a bonus to cross-functional teams that shorten the time it takes to bring new products to the Food and Drug Administration (FDA) for approval. "The plan they designed rewards the research and development group for developing viable concepts, testing them adequately and preparing the necessary documentation for the FDA. It emphasizes speeding up the process but only pays out if the quality remains high. For example, no awards are paid if the FDA returns the submissions for additional data that should have been included in the original package" (Huret, 1991, p. 40).

In another white-collar experiment, team awards are combined with individual bonuses (Eisman, 1990). At the Morris Savings Bank in New Jersey, employees each have a quarterly quota for things such as cross-selling and referrals, and they receive cash awards for each successful action. Each branch also has a quota for the total number of deposits per quarter. However, in order for an employee to receive a commission, both the branch and the employee must meet their quotas. As the branch results increase so do the bonuses received by each branch employee. Cross-functional teamwork is emphasized because the branch must succeed first before employees can receive their individual awards. However, individual effort is also recognized; the top salesperson of the quarter receives an extra bonus and managers of the top branches are given additional rewards.

In another bank, an incentive program directly encourages more cross-functional branch teamwork among all personnel including tellers, teller supervisors, customer service representatives, assistant managers, and branch managers (Elliott, 1991). The bank established goals in three areas: product sales, customer service, and profitability. In each area, measurable goals were defined (for example, the number of credit card applications) and each received a point value weighted in accordance with the bank's overall goals. Incentive dollars are paid to a branch based on the extent to which it reaches its quarterly goals. Cross-functional collaboration in the form of sharing ideas, pitching in, and helping each other out is fostered because no one employee gains anything unless the total team succeeds.

Dial Corporation, a leading soap and packaged-foods producer, recently tackled the tough problem of developing an incentive program that would reward cross-functional team selling (Murray, 1991). As in the previous examples, a mix of individual and team incentives was introduced. In 1989, the company reorganized into regional teams consisting of a marketing person, a financial specialist, and a customer service representative working in conjunction with the salespeople. Each region was designated a separate profit center with a bonus plan. Payouts are given semiannually based on both individual performance (results against goals) and on team results measured by sales volume, sales forecasting accuracy, and improved profitability.

Employee-Based Recognition Programs.   Thus far, we have talked about reward programs that are tied to some specific objective; when that objective is reached, the reward kicks in. However, it is also possible to reward cross-functional teams for some unplanned but extraordinary effort. Here is where a good recognition program can come into play. A small work group such as a department or region can reward individuals and teams that go beyond the expected performance. In addition, a recognition program can deal with the varied texture of employee motivation. Psychologists have told us for years that some people like to be recognized by an authority figure such as the boss while others only value acknowledgment from their colleagues and teammates. People also differ in the type of reward they enjoy. Some like public rewards, such as their name in the paper, while others prefer awards that are more "intrinsic," such as the opportunity to take on a new and challenging assignment.

The Language Standards Department of Bell Communications Research in Piscataway, New Jersey, a 120-person group of computer scientists, engineers, and support personnel operates a very successful, homegrown recognition program. While the reward criteria are quite general (for example, creativity, promotes teamwork, assistance to others, positive impact on clients), the nomination form insists that the nominator provide specific examples of how the criteria were met and what benefits were achieved. The selection committee includes the department director, one other manager, and five nonmanagement people plus the permanent volunteer secretary-facilitator. Thus, the selection is made by both peers and senior management, and the management and nonmanagement members of the committee change each quarter. In this way, over time, everyone has a chance to participate in the selection process. Awards, which are presented quarterly, may be given to both teams and individuals. The value of the award is approximately $150 per person; each person has a choice of gifts, such as dinner for two (up to $150), a gift certificate, desk accessories, a leather attaché case. Recipients also receive a certificate. In addition, their photo, along with a detailed description of their accomplishments, is posted on a prominent department bulletin board until the end of the quarter. The program includes a number of effective components:

- It allows the department to encourage and reward behavior that is consistent with its overall strategy, such as customer satisfaction and teamwork.

- Individuals and teams receive recognition both from their peers and from management.

- Everyone is eligible both to receive an award and to participate in the selection process.

- Everyone knows why the person or team was selected and therefore learns what behavior is valued in the department.

- The award is a noncash award of sufficient value to be coveted.

- The award provides the recipient with a choice of items and the chance to share the award with family and friends.

- The award has staying power because the pictures and descriptions of accomplishments remain on the bulletin board for three months.

Informal Team Recognition.   Not every department, branch, division, or company can establish a program for rewarding cross-functional teams — but every organization *can* recognize effective teams and positive team players. Recognition can take place every day and not cost a great deal of money nor require the establishment of a rewards program. Recognition is "free," or at least "low cost." In workshops, I often ask managers or team leaders to come up with a list of ways they can recognize teams or team players now, within their current budget, and without violating company policy. Participants are often amazed at how potentially empowered they are right now, although they rarely use all the authority they currently possess. They also do not use all their creativity. There is a great deal of recognition that can be accomplished without a formal program.

One simple but effective effort I especially liked was a regular column called In Appreciation, which appeared in a company newspaper. Each month, employees submitted items thanking other employees for those little extras. Here are some samples:

> To Dottie and D'Juana: Thank you for the blood, sweat, and tears (not to mention Saturdays and Sunday nights!) in helping to complete the report on time.
> —Don, Dave, Dean, Mary, and Mary Margaret

> To the Maintenance Department: Many thanks for your ongoing help in setting up the training room for the leadership classes. Your responsiveness and cheerfulness are greatly appreciated.
> —Terry

To Gene and his staff: Our efforts could not have been so successful without the help you and your department cheerfully and willingly gave us. Thanks much.
   — Research/Project CHAMPION

To the laboratory staff: Thanks for your continuous high-quality efforts.
   — Stan

Getting your name in the paper may appeal to you but not to someone else. Some teams prefer rewards that are external — that is, they appeal to what psychologists call extrinsic motivation. Other teams tend to be motivated by intrinsic rewards — those that appeal to the inner self of the team. In my experience, teams develop a character or style that is usually apparent, which makes it easy to determine the right type of recognition. But when in doubt, do some of both — that is, provide rewards that appeal to both types of motivation. The following lists present some ideas developed in brainstorming sessions with team leaders and managers in organizations. These lists provide a repertoire of recognition ideas that are available in most organizations.

Extrinsic Team-Recognition Ideas

1. Give verbal recognition at a staff meeting.

2. Ask the team to give a presentation at a staff meeting or company conference.

3. In a prominent location, display a poster with pictures, letters of commendation, and a description of team accomplishments.

4. Send the team on an outing (to a ball game, or on a boat ride, or other recreational activity).

5. Invite the team to your home for a barbecue.

6. Place a picture and story about the team in the company or community newspaper.

7. Encourage the team to speak at a professional conference.

8. Ask your boss to come to a team meeting to personally praise the team.

9. Send a letter to your boss about the work of the team.

10. Give each team member a T-shirt, hat, or mug with his or her name on it.

Intrinsic Team-Recognition Ideas

1. Ask the team to take on a tough problem or new challenge.

2. Provide timely, handwritten comments in the margin of documents prepared by the team.

3. Give the team the opportunity to work flexible hours, work at home, or have periodic off-site meetings.

4. Give the team new tools and other resources.

5. Ask the team for its opinion on a tough problem or new business opportunity.

6. Give the team the opportunity to learn a new system, operate some new equipment, or in other ways increase skills and knowledge.

7. Ask the team to help another team get started or solve a problem.

8. Make it clear you are implementing a team solution or in other ways using the results of the team's efforts.

9. Offer to pitch in and help the team directly, either by picking up some of the load, sharing your expertise, or helping to obtain outside assistance.

10. Empower the team to act in ways that will further its objectives.

In the end, it is the team itself that is best able to decide how it would like it and its members to be recognized. I often tell teams that if they wait for the organization to provide recognition, they may be very disappointed. Rather, they should plan and implement their own rewards program. If they have just launched a new product or program, deployed a new system, reduced turnaround time, decreased the number of customer complaints, or just had a good month, they should celebrate. Why not share a pizza for lunch, buy buttons or hats for everyone, or make up their own award certificate? How about a team awards meeting where "Oscars" are presented for such things as

- Most Valuable Player in a Supporting Role
- The Ralph Nader Award for Challenging the System (and living to tell about it)
- The US Air On Time–Every Time Award (for showing up on time to every meeting)
- The BFMA—Best Functional Manager Award—to the department manager who fully supported the work of the cross-functional team

The best recognition comes from being part of a successful effort and enjoying the work and the interaction with your colleagues. The daily forms of recognition that come from your teammates seem to be the most powerful and lasting. Here are some comments from cross-functional team members at a feedback meeting:

"I know you'll give me a straight answer."
"I respect your knowledge of computers."
"I like using you as a sounding board for my ideas."
"You have integrity."
"We need your sense of humor."

There are few more powerful forms of recognition than (1) really listening to what a person says and (2) asking another person for an opinion. When team members do these things with each other, everyone feels valued and rewarded for his or her participation on the team.

REWARDING CROSS-FUNCTIONAL TEAMWORK

There are relatively few rewards programs specifically designed for cross-functional teams. To design such a program, we must look to the work done in other areas, with standard work teams and broader group incentive systems. It is clear that a program must encourage, support, and reward the requirements for successful cross-functional teamwork. We must focus the rewards on such things as the coordination of all functions toward the achievement of team goals, the reduction of conflicts among departments, leadership that brings team members together, and results that come from the integration of diverse priorities.

1. *Team awards must reinforce the cross-functional team concept.* As was obvious in some of the examples cited in this chapter, none of us can win, unless we all win. A true team award requires the combined effort of team members representing all the related functions.

2. *Individual rewards must reinforce the cross-functional team concept.* Employees must get a consistent message that cross-functional teamwork is valued in the organization and will be rewarded. This message must be heard especially by the managers of functional departments who are sending people to these teams and by the service and support departments that the cross-functional teams often rely on to reach their goals.

As compensation experts Combs and Gomez-Meija point out (1991), "the single most important factor contributing to the relative integration of functional areas is the way rewards are allocated across these units. The compensation system and the particular mix of pay components used can send powerful signals to employees as to the organization's goals. If different signals are sent to the various functions,. . . coordination will suffer" (p. 45).

3. *Bring the reward down to the team level.* Most experts agree with the line-of-sight concept, in which the reward is clearly related to the team's performance. In other words, team members can see the relationship between their effort and the reward. In large organizations, gainsharing and profit-sharing programs are too far removed from the work of individual cross-functional teams. However, the team incentive programs described in this chapter for bank branches, regions, or departments demonstrate a clear relationship between team success and team rewards.

4. *Reward individual team players, too.* We still need to recognize individual team members who are outstanding team players—people who go beyond what is required and those who make an outstanding individual contribution to a team that is less than completely successful. For example, the Morris Savings Bank team incentive program described earlier in this chapter includes payoffs for employees who meet their individual quota, even when their branch does not receive a team award (Eisman, 1990).

In addition, we need to reward the coordinating cross-functional teams that we described in Chapter Five, which rarely engage in any real interdependent teamwork. These teams simply coordinate the efforts of individuals and departments. As team rewards experts Mower and Wilemon (1989) point out, "When the degree of interdependency among team members is low, team success depends mainly on each member's individual effort and ability. In such a situation, rewards may be most effective if they are distributed competitively and unequally, provided the basis for differentiation among members is perceived as fair" (p. 27). I am not sure I would use the word *competitively* to describe what is required, but I do agree that it is important to recognize individual team members who make important contributions to the total team effort.

5. *Use noncash rewards.* Many successful team incentive and recognition programs use merchandise and services as rewards in lieu of money. There is some disagreement about the value of noncash incentives. However, as my colleague

and rewards program expert Jerry McAdams of Maritz Corporation says, "Everyone wants more money, but studies continually show that people also want recognition for their contribution to the company" (Miller, 1991, p. 5).

McAdams sees a trend toward an increase in the use of noncash awards by companies (letter to the author, June 1993). With the current focus on quality, there is a need for awards that generate attention. Cash tends to get lost in the compensation process, but merchandise provides additional recognition. Noncash rewards last longer and are not perceived as compensation. The motivational value has a longer shelf life because each time employees use the briefcase, for example, they are reminded of how they obtained it. The item can also serve as a motivator to other people. Some noncash awards — such as dinner for two, a clock, a lawn mower — can be shared with family and friends. Most experts suggest including some other form of acknowledgment, such as a certificate or plaque, that is a permanent reminder of the accomplishment. The certificate, for example, can be displayed in an office or meeting room for others to see; perhaps it will motivate them as well. And finally, everyone agrees that "one size does not fit all." In other words, do not give every team member the same item. I like the use of a catalogue or a list of items having the same value. Then each team member can select the item that appeals.

6. *Use your arsenal of informal methods.* Do not wait for your company to establish a formal team incentive system or other program. As we indicated, much can be done on an informal, low-cost basis to recognize teams and team players. And in those situations where a formal program exists, use your insight into the needs of the teams to tailor your recognition efforts to them.

REWARDS AND
TEAM STRATEGY

Rewarding cross-functional teamwork is an important part of the overall team strategy. Although there are many rewards programs past and present to look to for models, it is clear that each organization must design a system that meets its unique needs. This chapter has presented examples from a variety of organizations to draw some specific conclusions about applications for cross-functional teams. The next chapter focuses on a potential benefit of cross-functional teamwork—team learning.

C H A P T E R

10

Learning as a
Team Event

*Our people must have the skills to work
across boundaries and units.
We are breaking up the company, but at the same time
we are focusing on putting it together,
both within units and between units.
Teamwork skills will be required.*
—Paul Allaire, Chairman and CEO, Xerox Corporation
(1992, p. 12)

Cross-functional teams provide an exciting opportunity for the creation of a learning community. As teams bring together scientists from different disciplines, craftspeople with different skills, employees from different functions, technical people with different specialties, the learning possibilities are almost limitless. A community of self-directed learners and teachers, with everyone playing both roles, is established. Colleagues and strangers can learn from each other in both formal and informal settings.

Technical Learning

On the surface, team learning focuses on the attainment of technical or information-based knowledge. Team members ask,

- As an electrical engineer, how can I learn about the tools of market research?
- As a machinist, how can I learn more about electrical wiring?
- As a geologist, how can I learn more about computer modeling?
- As a billing clerk, how can I learn more about processing claims?
- As a toxicologist, how can I learn more about dealing with regulatory agencies?

The team setting offers great opportunities for cross-functional learning. During team workshops, I ask participants to brainstorm a list of advantages of cross-functional teams for the individual team member. Without fail, "opportunities to learn" is high on the list. Many people view the opportunity to learn new things as a real benefit of team membership. Nowadays, people do not want to be stuck in the same job, doing the same thing, for their whole career. Not only is it that boring, but it also is not a smart career move. As we move toward the twenty-first century, the survivors will be employees with a broad-based technical background coupled with excellent problem-solving and interpersonal skills. In a reflective piece on the future of work in America, *Fortune* concluded: "Specialization is out, a new-style generalism is in. The most employable people will be flexible folk who can move easily from one function to another, integrating diverse disciplines and perspectives. Similarly, people who can operate comfortably in a variety of environments will fare better than those stuck in the mind-set of a particular corporate or even national culture. . . . People will need the ability not only to learn fundamentally new skills but also to *unlearn* outdated ways" (Sherman, 1993, p. 52, emphasis added).

INTERPERSONAL LEARNING

Team learning goes much beyond the exchange of technical knowledge and the ability to understand the jargon of other disciplines. Cross-functional teams provide team members with the opportunity to learn to work with a variety of different people. You can learn to understand the needs, values, and working styles of other people and, in the process, learn to work effectively with them. Team learning, therefore, involves the development of interpersonal skills and the establishment of a level of comfort in working with a diverse group of colleagues, strangers, and even old enemies. Adaptable interpersonal skills will be valued in the future as organizations make increasing use of cross-functional teams. The most prized employees will be people who can easily move from one team to the next and hit the ground running.

CROSS-CULTURAL LEARNING

Cross-functional teams are increasingly cross-cultural as well, as the work force in the United States becomes more culturally diverse. In some cases, cultural diversity is deliberately sought in the membership of the team. For example, in a recent team-building experience with a scientific team, it became clear that interpersonal conflict was the key issue. Although this was an American company, four of the six members of the team were born outside the United States. As a result, one of the underlying causes of conflict was a lack of understanding and appreciation of the cultural differences among team members. Team-building exercises brought out these differences as team members learned about each other and how their cultures influenced their teamwork styles.

In another team-building experience, the cross-functional team was composed of people based in different countries. The two primary countries, the United States and France, have very different business cultures. Americans tend to be informal, direct, and fast. The French, on the other hand, tend to be formal and like to take time to build relationships and arrive at a decision. In the process of participating on this team, members learned the nuances of the other culture and how to work most effectively in this cross-cultural environment. Beyond the immediate situation, team members also learned how to be effective in any transnational team. This ability to work with a diverse group of people will be valued more and more in the future, and the cross-functional team is an excellent place to learn how to do it.

PROBLEM-SOLVING LEARNING

There is something magical about the learning that can result from the interplay among the members of an effective cross-functional team. Viewing a problem or an opportunity from many angles can provide some exciting payoffs for the organization. For instance, a team is able to see possible changes on the horizon that may cause problems or provide opportunities for new products, systems, or services. In this way, cross-functional teams can be in the vanguard of the so-called adaptive organization. The adaptive organization is especially necessary in fast-changing markets, such as computers, where speed and flexibility are necessary for survival. Since cross-functional teams counter the rigidity of the bureaucratic functional organization, they can lead a change effort or at least respond quickly to opportunities.

Cross-functional teams also can be key players in the movement toward what Peter Senge calls generative learning organizations (Senge, 1990). While adaptive organizations are reactive to cues from the environment, generative organizations rely on imagination, vision, and dreaming about entirely new possibilities. These organizations go beyond asking customers what they want to creating something customers *might* want if they knew it were possible. By bringing together people from a variety of disciplines with diverse backgrounds and thinking styles, the cross-functional team increases the possibilities for generative learning—for creating new ideas, not by reshaping old ones but by fashioning them whole from new cloth.

CREATING THE TEAM LEARNING COMMUNITY

How does all this happen? Rarely does it happen in an organized educational sense. There are no classes, textbooks, or lectures. Rather, there is the creation of a learning environment—a culture that encourages exploration, risk taking, and openness to new ideas. Initially, the team leader is critical to successful team learning. One of my favorite leaders talks a great deal about vision and encourages those on his leadership team to join with him in creating a vision of the organization of the future. He also challenges the team with the need to look at the realities of the present, which can either help or hinder the team's journey toward the future. He is open to a variety of possibilities and encourages others on the team to think and act in creative new ways. He is also constantly exposing the team to new views of the world as seen by people outside of the company and the industry. In short, he is not afraid of new ideas. As a consequence, his team is a good example of a cross-functional team that is engaged in team learning—a place where people are continually learning and growing and using their learning to shape their future.

Training in Process Skills

Teamwork does not come naturally; working together in a team environment is a learned behavior. As Alfie Kohn (1986) has shown, competition is as American as apple pie, and often the emphasis on winning focuses on individual effort. We value individual excellence—the high scorer in the basketball game, the winning pitcher in the baseball game, the halfback who scores the winning touchdown. Even so-called team sports put a premium on individual performance. Little children, especially little boys, are encouraged to be the star of the team. The school system reinforces this behavior by pitting students against each other for grades and other forms of recognition. There is little emphasis on team learning. In fact, collaboration is often viewed as cheating. When groups of students are asked to work together on a school project, teammates often bicker about who did the most work and therefore who should get the best grade. Of course, things do not get much better in the business world, where performance appraisal is often a competitive exercise.

The net result of this scenario is that people need to be taught how to be effective team players and how to create effective teamwork. Programs for team leaders and members include a variety of process skills.

Understanding and Valuing Differences.   Team members need to develop an ability to appreciate and utilize the differences that define the cross-functional team. For example, in a cross-functional sales team, "technical people are seen as 'nerds' by sales people and technicians see sales people as 'Joe Isuzu' types. They must overcome the stereotypes and work toward mutual respect. Before good communication can occur, all team members must value the skills the other members bring to the team" (Hills, 1992, p. 57). In some cases, a training program has to overcome negative past experiences in cross-organizational collaboration or overcome negative perceptions of its members about people from other functions.

Being a Team Player.   In all training programs, people learn what it means to be a team player and how they can increase their personal effectiveness as team players. We start with the premise that effective teamwork comes from effective team players. Our research shows that there are many ways to be an effective team player (just as there are many ways to be an ineffective team player). To reiterate from an earlier chapter, there are four team player styles:

- *Contributor:* a task-oriented person who is good with details and enjoys supplying the team with specific technical data
- *Collaborator:* a goal-oriented member who pushes the team to fulfill its mission and is open to new ideas or methods for achievement
- *Communicator:* a process-oriented individual who is an effective listener and consensus builder
- *Challenger:* a person who questions the goals, methods, and ethics of the team and encourages the team to take well-conceived risks

These style differences can be a valuable resource for a cross-functional team. And since a cross-functional team is composed of people from different backgrounds, it is likely that it will have a diversity of team player styles among its members. Therefore, it is important that team members and leaders learn

- The strengths and weaknesses of each style
- Their personal style strengths and weaknesses
- How to increase their personal effectiveness as team players
- How to work effectively with team members with different styles

A survey instrument, the *Parker Team Player Survey* (Parker, 1991), can be used to determine team player styles.

Vision, Mission, Goals, and Roles. In the forming stage, teams need to develop a clear sense of purpose and an action plan, as well as clarity about the roles of team members. Chapter Six provides a model of goal setting for cross-functional teams that includes vision, mission, goals, objectives, and action plans. Teams, or sometimes just team leaders, learn the model and how to implement it with their team.

Conflict Resolution. By its very nature, a cross-functional team will have conflicts. Since the team is composed of people representing different styles, goals, priorities, expertise, and other factors, differences are endemic. There is nothing wrong with the existence of conflicts, only with the failure to satisfactorily resolve them. Teams need to (1) understand that differences are to be expected and even encouraged and (2) learn how to resolve differences in an effective manner. Here is an approach from my practice that seems to work:

> Prior to the team meeting, members each complete a self-assessment survey on how they resolve conflicts, and they complete a companion survey on each of their teammates. At the meeting, each person receives a confidential report summarizing the results of both surveys. The data are used to develop a personal development plan. In addition, the team identifies the causes of conflicts on the team and typical methods for conflict resolution. They then develop behavioral norms for resolving conflicts in the future. In a summary exercise, each member presents a list of personal "hot buttons" — the actions of others that set the team member off and lead to conflicts.

The above conflict survey was customized for a specific team based on its specific conflict issues, and it may not be appropriate for all teams. However, there are good commercial instruments available. The most popular and best-researched survey is the *Thomas-Kilmann Conflict Mode Instrument* (Thomas and Kilmann, 1974).

Team Meetings. Because quality and teamwork programs are growing by leaps and bounds, the number of meetings is growing also, to the point where a backlash can be expected. One of the best indicators of an imminent backlash in your organization is the number of times you hear the phrase, "I can't get my work done because I'm always in a meeting." I believe negative reactions like this are not directed at the validity of the teamwork effort but at the many ineffective meetings that take place. If you want to get depressed, calculate the cost of a meeting in your organization by simply multiplying the average hourly rate of the participants by the length of the meeting. At that point, you may begin to provide training and guidelines for how to plan and manage meetings.

Cross-functional teams have some special meeting management problems. Since team members are not used to working together, they may not have a set of common procedures and norms for team meetings. Lack of common understandings can lead to conflicts. For example, one of the problems that comes up on cross-functional teams is the starting time of the meeting. Some people are very precise while others are quite cavalier about being punctual. Comments such as "You know those marketing people, they never show up on time" or "You can bet the ranch that the engineers will throw a fit if we start the meeting more than five minutes after the announced time" reflect the style differences that are part of the culture of a cross-functional team. One way I deal with this issue is to have the team establish a set of meeting norms as early as possible in the life cycle of the team.

Another issue often associated with cross-functional teams is the frequency of team meetings. When the team is large or members are located in many different sites, face-to-face meetings are not held very often. As a result, when a team meeting takes place, it is crucial to use the time effectively. Good skills for planning and facilitating meetings are at a premium.

Such skills are not difficult to learn. Above all, meeting management requires discipline. It is important to know what to do, and just as important, to do it every time. There are several good books on meetings (Kieffer, 1988; 3M Meeting Management Team, 1979; Doyle and Strauss, 1976), so it is not necessary here to provide a complete protocol. However, some points are especially important for training cross-functional teams:

- Develop a set of norms or guidelines for team meetings that reflect the diversity of the team's membership.

- Plan the meeting carefully, including the preparation of an agenda that provides an accurate estimate of the time and action required for each item.

- Provide some opportunity for relationship building by including such things as subgrouping during the meeting, coffee time prior to the meeting, or a social period afterwards.

- Where available and appropriate, train a facilitator to help plan and conduct the process aspects of the meeting.

For more specific advice on cross-functional team meetings, see Chapter Twelve.

Team Building.   The most useful developmental activity for cross-functional teams is team building. In other words, the entire team goes through an experience together. For example, I offer my clients a course entitled Increasing the Effectiveness of Cross-Functional Teams. Employees who are also on cross-functional teams may sign up for it individually. The hope is that they will go back to their teams and apply the new information. However, that can be a stretch, since other team members have not had the same course. Therefore, attending the course remains an educational experience ("I now know what makes a cross-functional team successful"). The course is also offered to cross-functional teams who want to attend the course as a team. In this format, they can simultaneously learn and apply the new information to their team. For example, they learn the success factors for cross-functional teams and then see how their team stacks up against these criteria. Based on this exercise the team then devises an action plan to increase their effectiveness. The net result of the program is powerful—the team leaves with increased knowledge about cross-functional teams and a shared plan for growth and development of their team.

Leader Training. As we indicated in Chapter Four, cross-functional teams have special leadership needs that are distinct from other teams. Separate training for the leaders of cross-functional teams is often desirable. A leader training workshop often covers the following:

- *The Role of the Leader:* How to provide both technical and process leadership; operate with unclear or little authority; maintain external relations; deal with diverse team player styles; resolve conflicts

- *Creating a Vision and Setting Goals:* How to provide vision and engage the team in a process of collaborative goal setting

- *Stakeholder Analysis:* How to identify the team's key stakeholders and develop plans for working effectively with them

- *Managing Meetings:* How to plan and conduct team meetings

- *Communication Skills:* How to understand and develop a personal style and techniques for communicating with a diverse membership

- *Problem Situations:* How to analyze and solve typical cross-functional team problems

Technical Training

One of the assumed benefits of cross-functional teams is the opportunity for cross-training. Thus far, successful cross-training has been limited to shop-floor teams and customer service positions in offices. One of the best-known experiments is taking place at Aid Association for Lutherans (AAL), a company that sells life and health insurance to a mainly Lutheran customer base (Kaeter, 1993). Several years ago, the company shifted the focus of the staff who served the field sales representatives from that of functional management to that of a team-based cross-functional organization. In essence, that meant going from a situation where one person handled only one function, such as new applications, to a team approach where every team member can handle any request from a sales rep. There are many benefits of this approach but the most significant are that the salesperson does not get bumped from one person to the next, requests are handled faster, and fewer mistakes are made. Obviously, the only way to make this system work is to train each team member in how to handle all the required functions. AAL relied primarily on one-on-one training (team members taught each other); later the company found that some formal classroom instruction was necessary to fill in some gaps in knowledge. However, what made the whole thing work was a pay-for-knowledge system, which rewarded team members with additional compensation as they learned and then applied the new information on the job. (See Chapter Nine for a description of knowledge-based pay systems.)

Many companies are creating self-directed cross-functional teams at the shop-floor level. Wherever it makes sense, companies are reducing the number of job classifications and then are cross-training team members. Cross-training gives the organization the flexibility to speed up the existing process ("We don't have to wait for an electrician to show up") and to move quickly to shift to another product line in response to an order. Motorola, Corning, and General Motors are among the many companies who are using the flexibility of cross-trained teams to improve their business.

Cross-training on scientific and technical cross-functional teams has been limited to presentations at team meetings and informal, self-directed, one-on-one learning. And yet, "One of the prime requirements for effective interdisciplinary interaction is that all members should have an understanding and appreciation of the contributions from other disciplines. This includes understanding their attitudes and values, as well as their technical skills" (Pearson, 1983, p. 391). It is true that some professionals do not want to share their knowledge, fearing that they will thereby decrease their value to the organization. We must help people get beyond this, perhaps by rewarding them for sharing their expertise and helping them understand the value of their knowledge to the success of the team. In the future, the training of cross-functional teams must include cross-training in technical knowledge and skills. However, it's important to understand what this type of technical training is and is not.

A market research specialist will never become a fully trained toxicologist, but he or she can learn enough to ask intelligent questions about the product that may help with the formulation of the overall team strategy. An engineer may never fully grasp the psychological implications of a proposed product enhancement, but she or he could learn enough to help tailor the specifications to the targeted consumer. If these teams are to be successful, cross-training will be synonymous with cross-functional teamwork.

STRATEGIES FOR
TEAM LEARNING

Facilitating Informal Team Learning

Team leaders can encourage the informal learning that should be so much a part of the natural dynamics of a cross-functional team. In discussions at team meetings, the leader can seek a wide range of opinion about a topic. Too often, members feel they can only speak about agenda topics that fall within their recognized area of expertise; in other words, scientists can only discuss the scientific issues while marketing representatives should restrict remarks to the market potential of a product. Leaders need to help team members take a broader view of the potential for learning in a team setting by encouraging opinions from everyone. Other approaches such as off-site team meetings and informal sessions before and after team meetings often help break down these rigid barriers and open up learning possibilities.

Training Team Leaders and Team Members

Organizations that demonstrate a serious commitment to cross-functional teamwork provide training workshops for both leaders and members. It cannot be expected that people will come to the team with the required skills. The specific subjects and methodologies for team training described in this chapter need to be taught.

Fostering Team Building

If we have learned one thing about the development of teams, it is that providing training and development for whole teams is clearly the most effective strategy. When the team goes through the experience together, they are immediately able to apply what they've learned. The outcomes are more likely to be sustained.

Supporting Technical Training

I see team members asking, pleading, and demanding to know more about the work of others. They see technical training both as a personal benefit and an enhancement of the team process. The best way to institute team-based technical training is to have team members teach each other. Each team member is better able to tailor the training to the needs of their teammates than some specialist from outside the team. In addition, team members will begin to see each other as valued resources.

The development of a team learning community works best in a small, informal environment. Large teams make it difficult to obtain the benefits of team training described in this chapter. The next chapter tackles the issue of team size and suggests methods for dealing with large teams.

11

Gaining the Power
of Small Teams

Bigger isn't always better, especially when it comes to cross-functional teams. In the drive for participation and involvement, many organizations have sought to demonstrate their commitment by making a team member out of every last person with some connection to the task. It's a high price to pay for trying to make sure people do not feel left out. The net result is that teams have grown in size but decreased in productivity, and team members have no real sense of involvement beyond having their name on the team roster. I have seen cross-functional project teams in the telecommunications and pharmaceutical industries with twenty, thirty, or even fifty members, even though we know that groups that large are just not effective.

THE ALLURE
OF LARGE TEAMS

For some organizations, bigger does indeed seem to feel better, if not actually be better. Why? The answers vary:

1.   More team members means more ideas.

2.   The bigger the team, the more important the project.

3.   A big team means my job as team leader must be big and important.

4.   We can't leave anyone out.

5.   Team meetings are a good educational forum. They provide a good opportunity to orient and train junior staffers.

1. *More team members means more ideas.* Having more team members does provide the potential for more ideas. We emphasize *potential* because it does not often translate into reality. Of six studies that examined the effects of group size on idea generation, only one found larger groups to generate more ideas than smaller groups (Hackman and Vidmar, 1970; Bouchard and Hare, 1970; Bouchard, Draden, and Barasaloux, 1974; Renzulli, Owen, and Callahan, 1974; Lewis, Sadosky, and Connolly, 1975; Fern, 1982).

The clear conclusion is that while large groups bring more minds to bear on a problem, not all of the minds actually contribute ideas. Small groups encourage participation because more people feel free to speak up. The net result is more ideas come out in small groups.

2. *The bigger the team, the more important the project.* It is true that people often associate the relative importance of a project with the size of the team. In other words, if it's big it must be important. In addition, the team of an important project tends to get bigger because more people want to be on the team. A hot, visible project tends to draw people who want to be "where the action is." Unfortunately, one of the best ways

to ensure the failure of an important project team is to allow its membership to grow beyond a small, solid working group. All research studies on group size show that as the size of the group increases, per person productivity decreases.

3. *A big team means my job as team leader must be important.* Some team leaders have the view that if they have a big team with a big budget then they themselves must be important. Imagine how good it must sound to say, "I head the Polymers Team, which has forty-five members from across the division." While that can be a major ego trip for some team leaders, it will be short-lived if the team produces little of real value to the organization. And unless the team uses some effective subgrouping, it is not likely to produce anything of value. The team leader would be better advised to reduce the size of the team, thereby increasing its chances of being successful. In the end, it will sound a great deal more impressive to say, "I was leader of the Polymers Project Team, which brought that new heavy-duty adhesive to the market in less than eighteen months."

4. *We can't leave anyone out.* This can be one of the most seductive arguments. Aren't we looking for more participation and involvement? Don't we want various departments to support the team? Shouldn't anyone who wants to participate be allowed to participate? While we do want involvement and support, it does not require the direct participation of every last person to achieve that end. In fact, as a cross-functional team increases in size beyond ten members, an individual's opportunity and ability to effectively participate decreases dramatically. So although you have not been "left out," you are not really "in." We have included you on the team's roster of members and meeting distribution list but your opportunity to be an active team player is more symbolic than substantive.

5. *Team meetings are a good educational forum.* Many managers use project team meetings as an opportunity to orient new employees and provide a broadening educational experience for junior staffers. Employees are sent to team meetings, not to participate but to observe, learn, and often to take notes and report back to the department. There is no

question that team meetings are educational. You can learn about the topic being explored as well as how cross-functional teams operate. However, there are many problems with this approach. First, let's be honest—some managers and senior staff members simply do not want to go to these team meetings. In these cases, sending junior people to the meetings for the "educational value" is suspect. Second, making team meetings a positive educational experience requires that the person attend meetings on a regular basis, not just when a senior person does not feel like going; the person have some background on the subject or be briefed before the meeting; and the person have an opportunity to ask questions and clarify issues that come up at the meeting. Unfortunately, these criteria are rarely met. Finally, and perhaps more important, the cross-functional team does not benefit from the attendance of these outside people. In fact, their presence may detract from team effectiveness by simply increasing the number of noncontributing bodies in the room.

AN INCREASE IN TEAM SIZE = A DECREASE IN PRODUCTIVITY

Researchers who study team productivity have concluded that as team membership increases, the individual productivity of team members decreases, because members are spending more of their time communicating about the task to others. Louis Fried, vice president of information technology for SRI International, who has studied project teams, found that "in groups of five members or less, such task-oriented communication can consume from 10 percent to 30 percent of each member's time. As the number of people in the group increases beyond five, members must spend more of their time communicating and may eventually reach an upper limit of approximately 90 percent" (Fried, 1991, p. 28). Fried concludes that "with every team member added, the communication load increases and the net productivity of each team member decreases" (p. 29).

AN INCREASE IN TEAM SIZE = A DECREASE IN TEAM MEMBER ACCOUNTABILITY

Just about every study of team size shows that as the number of team members increase, participation, trust, and accountability decrease. *Social loafing* is a term psychologists use to describe the reduction in individual effort as the size of the team increases. The so-called loafing occurs because the more people there are on your team, the less responsible you feel for the team's success, since there are other people around to pick up the slack. However, when you feel your performance is being closely monitored by your teammates, you are more likely to be concerned about how they evaluate you. As a result, you are more likely to produce than you are on larger teams, where you can get "lost in the crowd." In general, the larger the team, the more you feel that your responsibilities can be diffused. The smaller the team, the more you feel responsible to produce.

AN INCREASE IN TEAM SIZE = A DECREASE IN PARTICIPATION AND TRUST

Two additional concerns with large teams are participation and trust. The more members a team has, the more likely it will be that a few strong personalities will dominate discussions and the decision-making process. Many potentially good team players will remain passive, hesitant to voice their good ideas and opinions in front of a large group. This phenomenon is likely to kick in as the team exceeds eight or nine members.

The level of trust on a team, always a key issue, tends to decrease as the group size increases (Sato, 1988). As the size of the team increases, members are less likely to

- Be open and honest in their comments
- Be willing to disagree with the leader
- Feel confident that they can depend on each other
- Give each other honest feedback

OPTIMAL TEAM SIZE

It is not surprising that the perceptions of managers support the results of studies by empirical researchers. Although optimal size will depend on the specific team mission, in general, optimal team size is four to six members, with ten to twelve being the maximum for effectiveness. The following are some typical views on the size of cross-functional teams:

> Our goal is to get all interested parties involved. If fifteen parties are users, I invite a representative sample of those parties to work on the team, but then give everyone a chance to review the recommendations. We call the small group a core team.
> —Bill Hines, Executive Director, Bell Communications Research (interview with the author, January 1993)

> The size of the team is based on the issue, but it is typically in the range of six to eight people.
> —Naomi Marrow, Director, Human Resources, Reader's Digest (interview with the author, January 1993)

Our teams are large, sometimes as large as eighty people. The total team meets periodically to review status reports. However, the working group is a core team of about eight people, who are usually also the chairs of the various subgroups of the team. The subgroup is where most of the real work gets done.
    — Jose Verger, Product Manager, Pacific Bell (interview with the author, January 1993)

Eight to ten is the best size.
    — Jim Kochanski, Director, Human Resources, Northern Telecom (interview with the author, January 1993)

For work teams, that is teams doing real work, team size is first determined by the required interdependence of the task. Team effectiveness is then considered, and eight to twelve people is the usual size.
    — Stuart Winby, Director, Hewlett-Packard (interview with the author, February 1993)

Large teams are broken down into subteams. I recommend eight per team.
    — Alf Higginbotham, Maritime Life Assurance Company (survey response)

Teams should be limited to no more than a dozen people. Beyond that you begin to lose the ability to communicate and work closely as a team.
    — Mike McGrath, Managing Director, Pittiglio, Rabin, Todd and McGrath (Whiting, 1991, p. 51)

STRATEGIES FOR TEAM SIZE

What should you do? There is simply no getting around the fact that small teams work best. Following are some ideas that a variety of organizations are using successfully.

Playing Hardball: Limiting the Size of Your Team

Do the right thing. You know that large teams do not work well. When new teams are formed, insist that they include less than ten members, or use the core team concept or use subgroups. Reorganize existing teams into smaller units. One major pharmaceutical company, Rhone-Poulenc Rorer, recently slashed the size of its large project (drug development) teams into small, working teams. Team leaders are free to invite other subject-matter experts to assist as the need arises. It was not easy to eliminate people from some teams, but the long-term impact on the teams and the development process will be salutary.

Using the Core Team Approach

A core team is a cross-functional team consisting of representatives of the functions critical to the achievement of the team's goals. Typical core teams include from five to eight members. For example, a core team at Sun Microsystems responsible for the development of a new workstation included the team leader and representatives from software engineering, hardware engineering, operations, customer service and support, marketing, and finance. The core team provides the leadership and makes the key decisions for the project. Sometimes it does much of the real work; more often, however, it meets regularly with people in the functional area who support (that is, who do the work for) the team, to ensure that the work conforms to quality standards and is on time. In some organizations, core team members also serve as leaders of the functional teams.

Dividing into Subgroups

An old group dynamics tactic is to break up large teams into small working groups. Many leaders of cross-functional teams, faced with the "political" necessity of having a large team, have skillfully used subcommittees to achieve the advantages of small groups. In this model, the full team meets monthly (or maybe only quarterly) to review the status reports of the subcommittees. The subcommittees provide a real opportunity for team members to utilize their expertise and have an impact on the outcome. Participation is limited to technical work because decisions on the mission and critical project direction are usually made by the leader and a small cadre of influential members.

SMALL IS BEAUTIFUL AND BETTER

Cross-functional teams seem to be particularly prone to the problem of getting too large to be effective. In an effort to avoid offending both allies and enemies, team sponsors simply add people from the various functional areas to the team. They do this despite the fact that both common sense and research data say that smaller is better. A recent major study of fifty teams in a variety of industries concluded that "large numbers of people usually cannot develop the common purpose, goals, approach, and mutual accountability of a real team. And when they do so, they usually produce only superficial 'missions' and well-meaning intentions" (Katzenbach and Smith, 1993b, p. 47).

In this chapter, I have provided some techniques for dealing with team size. In the next chapter, I explore a variety of techniques for providing the positive internal dynamics of a successful cross-functional team.

C H A P T E R

12

Techniques for Working Together as a Team

There are a number of internal issues that affect the success of cross-functional teams. These issues are

1. *Conflict Resolution:* the ability of the team to discuss and resolve differences

2. *Open Communication and Trust:* the degree to which team members feel free to express their views

3. *Managing Meetings:* the team's ability to plan and conduct effective meetings

4. *Characteristics of Team Members:* the capabilities and styles of team members

5. *Customers and Suppliers:* the degree to which the team effectively partners with suppliers and customers

6. *Colocation:* the relative importance of physical proximity as a facilitator of team communication

7. *Communications Technology:* the degree to which the team has access to and uses technology to enhance team communications

It is possible to look at these issues and think that they apply equally to any type of team. Of course, the ability to effectively manage the internal dynamics is important to the success of all teams. However, each of these areas presents special problems for cross-functional teams, and each requires a solution tailored to the unique characteristics of a team composed of people from a variety of functions with a myriad of past relationships.

CONFLICT RESOLUTION

As the traditional hierarchical organization gives way to a horizontal division of labor dominated by technical specialists, conflicts on teams will become even more prevalent. In fact, if we define conflicts as simply differences of opinion, this is exactly what we want to happen. In bringing together a diverse group of experts, we expect and want these differences to surface because, in the end, we expect a better outcome to result. As McCorcle (1982) has pointed out, for cross-functional teams, "a prime advantage over other types of groups is their diversity of members. Ideally, each person brings a specific set of skills and a unique perspective to the problem at hand" (p. 296). However, he goes on to note that this diversity can become a barrier to success. "Though such a group may have the potential to bring expertise to bear on a wide range of problems . . . it might also face serious difficulty in working as a unit. . . . It is not because group members might refuse to work together, but because in such a group each person (or represented discipline) could have different ideas about the best way to solve a given problem" (p. 296). If the team is composed of people with different priorities, different team player styles, and some past negative experiences in working together, conflicts will naturally arise.

Conflicts and Performance

These built-in conflicts can lead to poor performance. Ancona and Caldwell's (1991) study of cross-functional new-product teams suggests that "high levels of functional diversity are directly associated with lower levels of performance, particularly for management ratings of innovation and for teams' ratings of their own performance" (p. 14). Assessments of performance can be deceptive. Since the use of cross-functional teams is relatively new, expectations can be high and standards of success can lack uniformity. In many situations, it was assumed that simply bringing together experts from a variety of disciplines would produce tangible, high-quality results in less time. The power of the idea of cross-functional teamwork obscured the conflicts inherent in the design of the team. As a result, in many cases, expectations were unrealistic. Management expected cycle time to be reduced, product quality to be improved rapidly, and customer service to be upgraded immediately. Team members expected the team to run smoothly right from the start.

Cross-functional teams do produce conflicts among members. In fact, we expect it and want it, but these differences take time and skill to resolve. However, teams are rarely warned about the potential for conflict or trained to effectively resolve the differences. Therefore, when management and team members are asked to assess the team's performance, they are dissatisfied because their expectations were not met. They see team conflict and the time it takes to resolve the conflict as a negative feature; therefore, they are less than completely satisfied with the results. They fail to understand that conflicts are to be expected and valued. They also do not appreciate that the time invested up front in exploring these differences can lead to saving time and improving quality down the line. As Elizabeth Culotta (1993) has noted in her report on cross-functional scientific teams, conflicts are seen as positive because disagreements among team members point to problems in the research that need to be fixed.

Dealing with Team Conflict

The unique nature of cross-functional teams requires some methods for handling the conflict that is central to the existence of any such team.

1. As I suggest in Chapter Ten, team training must include sessions on conflict resolution. Team members and leaders must learn that conflicts are to be expected and even valued. However, they must also learn to be open to new ideas and develop skills in listening, questioning, and consensus building.

2. Top management as well as functional department managers must be oriented to the characteristics of cross-functional teams. These managers must also be helped to form realistic expectations about the potential outcomes of cross-functional teams.

3. In some cases, teams may need to get expert help in facilitating team processes. Some companies use human resource professionals while other organizations use co-leaders who have been trained in group process. For example, TRW in Cleveland taps high-potential people, trains them in facilitation skills, and then has them help facilitate teams in other areas.

OPEN COMMUNICATION AND TRUST

Trust is the pathway to open communication; its absence can undermine a team's effectiveness. On some cross-functional teams, conflicts exist but do not surface because members do not feel free to express their opinions or share their expertise.

For example, whenever a corporate culture makes people "level conscious," open communication may be limited when team members include different management levels as well as nonmanagement employees. Lower-level employees are afraid to speak up; as one person told me, "If you say the wrong thing, it is used against you." In another case, when I asked a cross-functional team member why she didn't disagree with a particular point, she said, "Oh, I wouldn't disagree with him, he's got too many Hay points."

Lack of trust can also be high in cross-functional teams that are cross-level as well. In her study of a cross-functional project team, Linda Loehr (1991) found that "the lack of trust among team members constrained their individual and collective voices, restricting the sharing of knowledge, experience and opinions. . . . Indications of mistrust among nonmanagerial team members ranged from mistrust of the worth of their ideas to mistrust of the system that required their generation" (p. 53).

Poor communication on cross-functional teams also occurs on teams that do not have significant differences in levels. Strangers do not immediately trust each other. Antagonists from past wars may feel suspicious or resentful. Others may simply take a wait-and-see attitude.

Factors in Poor Communications

Some of the factors that lead to poor communication among cross-functional team members include the following:

- Lack of appreciation of the contributions of other functions. For example, in telecommunications projects, some engineers do not value the input provided by human factors psychologists.
- Plain old-fashioned turf battles. Some departments play out their competitive games on the field provided by the cross-functional team.
- Different jargon. For example, line department users often do not understand the terminology and technology employed by computer programmers.

- Different work orientations. For example, researchers tend to take a long-term view and have an informal work climate; operations people are more short term and formal; salespeople are usually informal and have a short-term focus. While one may argue with these generalizations, it is clear that each department or function develops it own work style, which may clash with other styles from other functions.
- Different degrees of interest in the team's outcome. Some cross-functional team members are simply more interested in the team's purpose and may have more to gain from a successful outcome. In one government agency, team members from one bureau have more interest in the outcome of the team because it affects their client group more than it does the other bureaus represented on the team.
- Mistaken goals. Some team members mistakenly see harmony as the goal of cross-functional teamwork. As a result, they are afraid to express a contrary point of view for fear that it will destroy the positive feelings among team members. The net result is a false consensus and a less than satisfactory outcome.

While these factors explain lack of trust and communication on cross-functional teams, they do not excuse it. Members of cross-functional teams are there because they have something to contribute. They must be allowed and even encouraged to share their ideas, information, and opinions without restrictions. Open communication is an absolute requirement for successful cross-functional teamwork. The concept of the cross-functional team is that the outcome—the product, the system, the service—will be better because it has been created by the combined expertise of people from a variety of functions. Viewing a problem or an issue from many vantage points is the strength of the cross-functional team. However, the value of divergent views can only be realized when there is a free flow of information.

Establishing Communication Guidelines

In working with cross-functional teams, we encourage the establishment of guidelines on communication and trust. A team's list of norms will often include such things as:

- All ideas are given a fair hearing.
- Everyone will have an opportunity to contribute information and opinions.
- Open and honest opinions are welcome.
- Members are expected to actively listen to each other.
- Rank does not have its privilege.

MANAGING MEETINGS

As noted in Chapter Ten, effective meetings are especially important for cross-functional teams. When you bring together a group of people who have different skills, diverse experiences, a variety of work styles, and often conflicting priorities, the process of managing the interactions can be tricky at best. As much as we hate meetings, they are still the principal vehicle for team actions and the most visible aspect of a team's operation. It is where the conflicts and communication get played out.

The Meeting Monsters
Cross-functional teams seem to be susceptible to a number of what might be called "meeting monsters."

Too Many Meetings.   Many people erroneously believe that the only place to get any teamwork done is in a meeting. Wrong! This belief is the chief contributor to the antiteamwork, antiquality backlash that is starting to mushroom. But since many meetings are so poorly conducted, people associate bad meetings with quality and teamwork and are ready to give up on all three. The best way to eliminate this monster is simply to eliminate unnecessary meetings. Here's how:

1.   Change your orientation. Instead of believing that all teamwork must take place in meetings, realize that not everything requires a face-to-face meeting.

2. Meet only when you have a clear purpose for meeting. A regular weekly team meeting may not be necessary. The simple rule is: *No purpose, no meeting!*
3. Meet only when the time is right. Once you have a clear purpose, the time may still not be right because
    ▪ All the required information or equipment is not available
    ▪ All the key players are not available
    ▪ An appropriate meeting facility is not available
    ▪ An important organizational change is about to be announced
4. Consider other possible alternatives. If the purpose of your meeting is to communicate information, why not use voice or electronic mail, the fax, or the local area network; or distribute paper reports; or meet separately with each person.
5. Ask yourself: What would happen if the meeting were not held? If the answer is nothing, or "There would be a loud cheer throughout the organization," then you definitely do not hold the meeting.

Too Much Time in Meetings.   There are several reasons meetings last too long. First, the agenda contains too many items. Second, not enough time has been allocated for each agenda item. Third, the agenda and the time limits are not followed. The best way to keep the length of the meeting reasonable is by good, solid, premeeting planning. Begin by clarifying the purpose of the meeting and then include only those items that pertain to the purpose. Handle other items, such as communicating progress reports and other similar information, in the ways suggested above (voice mail, fax, and so on). Then add time limitations to each agenda item. During the meeting, remind team members about the time limits and try to stay within them. If you are going over the limits, either refer the item to a subcommittee or ask the team whether they want to take more time with this item and eliminate others.

Too Many People at Meetings. Cross-functional teams seem particularly susceptible to this monster. Many of the teams are either just too large to begin with or they allow visitors and observers to attend team meetings. One way to reduce the number is to have the meeting notice designate "required" attendees and "optional" attendees. At the meeting, seat the required or core team members around the table to facilitate discussion and decision making. Ask the other people to sit around the perimeter.

Not Enough Done at Meetings. This is the most frustrating problem of cross-functional team management. Since expectations are high and so much seems to be riding on the meeting, lack of action is especially detrimental to team morale. The management of the meeting requires good group process skills, which unfortunately many cross-functional team leaders do not possess. As we have said, good process skills are needed because a cross-functional team brings together people who have different working styles and little experience in working together. We have suggested providing either training for team leaders or an experienced facilitator to assist the leader. In the absence of either, here are some useful tips for conducting a team meeting:

1. Start on time. Need we say more?
2. Open the meeting with a brief statement of the purpose and a review of the agenda and time limits.
3. Follow the agenda. Begin the discussion with, "We've allocated thirty minutes to this item." Intervene during the discussion with, "Let's move on. We only have ten minutes more for this subject." If someone wants to bring up another subject, ask them to wait until the item is discussed later in the meeting, or made an agenda item at the next meeting, or given to a committee for consideration.
4. Manage the discussion. Use facilitative comments or questions that move the team along.
    - Ask for opinions: "How do you react to...?"
    - Involve participants: "Can marketing live with this new approach?"

- Clarify ideas: "In other words, you feel we should talk directly to the customer."
- Stay focused: "We were discussing data collection. What other approaches can we use?"
- Summarize: "OK, it looks as if the feedback is telling us that..."
- Test for consensus: "We seem to be saying that we want to..."
- Explore differences: "At this point, the operations folks feel that... while engineering can only do..."
- Take action: "We have agreed to.... What steps do we need to take to get started?"

5. Summarize the meeting. When the agenda has been completed, the leader should close the meeting by briefly summarizing the key decisions and next steps.
6. Confirm action items. As part of the meeting, the action items should be confirmed. Each action item should specify (1) the action required, (2) the person responsible, and (3) the due date.

CHARACTERISTICS OF TEAM MEMBERS

Teamwork starts with you and me. It begins with the individual—the team player. You cannot have effective teamwork without effective team players and, more important, without a *diverse* group of effective team players. As many organizations reorganize into cross-functional teams, the opportunity to select the best mix of team players is presented. What then are the characteristics of team members that are especially relevant to cross-functional teams?

Technical Expertise

There is no getting around the need for people who "know their cookies." The team needs information, skill, and expertise to solve problems and make decisions. However, there is more to the story. Technical expertise must be coupled with the willingness and ability to share the expertise. This is the key characteristic of the team player type I call the Contributor. While the willingness to share your expertise may seem obvious, it is not universally practiced. Some experts see their knowledge as a source of power and a factor that differentiates them in the organization. As a result, they either withhold information or make it difficult for others to use. On the other hand, the effective Contributor freely shares the information in a form easily understood by others and is willing to serve as a mentor and trainer of team members from other areas.

Technical expertise should be linked with an ability to communicate with team members in other disciplines, who lack the same technical background as the expert. It is not enough to know your subject; to be effective on the team, you must be able to communicate your expertise so that it can be easily understood by other team members. I recently overheard a team member say, "I didn't realize that you were not technical." This was a not so subtle put-down delivered to another team member who asked questions during a presentation. My reaction to that comment is that it was the responsibility of the presenter of the information to communicate effectively with nontechnical team members. I know some very good technical experts who are able to communicate with just about anyone because they understand the audience and can translate their ideas into analogies and other forms easily understood by others.

Openness to New Ideas

Cross-functional teams bring together people from a variety of disciplines. As a team member, you must be able to do more than just share your ideas — you must also be willing to listen to and consider the views of others, even when those views differ from yours. The willingness to be open to new and different ideas is critical because it is the very behavior that allows the team to take advantage of the unique nature of the cross-functional team. In other words, there is no sense bringing together all these people with different ideas if members do not give adequate consideration to each other's ideas.

I refer to this type of team player as the Communicator. This person should also have the ability to help the team synthesize the various points of view.

Willingness to Ask Tough Questions

Since we value the need for open communication on a cross-functional team, we need to have team members who will raise questions about the team's work and disagree with other team members, including the team leader. I call this team player a Challenger. In Loehr's study of a cross-functional project team, the failure of team members to disagree in a constructive manner during team meetings greatly diminished the team's effectiveness (Loehr, 1991). Team members had opinions, which they shared with the researcher in private interviews, but were reluctant to express them during team meetings. While the team has to establish and enforce norms about open communication, it is helpful to stock the team with effective Challengers.

Ability to See the Big Picture

Since the cross-functional team can get bogged down in the details of data, studies, field trials, and other nitty-gritty things, the team needs someone who can provide vision. The Collaborator is the team player who helps the team set overarching goals and put its work into the proper organizational context. Periodically, the team needs to remember why it exists and where it is heading.

Awareness of Cultural Diversity

The population of the United States is changing and people from other cultures, as well as women, are becoming a larger percentage of the work force. Increasingly, cross-functional teams are reflecting these changes by becoming cross-cultural too, and team members have to be able to work with people from other cultures. In Chapter Ten I described a team composed of six people, four of whom were born outside the United States. Many of the conflicts on the team stemmed from the members' lack of knowledge of each other's culture and its impact on participation on the team. When team members discussed their family and cultural background, they were better able to understand each other's behavior and to improve their interpersonal communication.

In another organization (also mentioned in Chapter Ten), the new-product development team included representatives from at least three different countries. The language barriers were among the easiest hurdles to overcome, but the cultural differences presented the biggest challenges. The team members from France come from what is called a high-context culture, while members from the United States typically represent a low-context culture (Halverson, 1992). Americans like to move quickly, to get down to work, and to make decisions in the meeting. The French, on the other hand, like to take time to build relationships and establish trust before proceeding to the business at hand. Cross-functional, cross-cultural teams like this one need to adjust some of their meeting management techniques to accommodate the needs of all team members. For example, earlier in this chapter we recommended starting meetings on time, getting right down to business, and sticking to the agenda. This approach favors people from low-context cultures but does not meet the needs of high-context team members, who might want to spend time at the beginning of the meeting (or over coffee prior to the meeting) socializing with their colleagues.

CUSTOMERS AND SUPPLIERS

As organizations begin to see work as a process, with suppliers at one end and customers at the other, teamwork with suppliers and customers becomes the most natural thing to do. In addition, as companies experiment with certification of suppliers, reduce the number of suppliers, and go to single-source suppliers, it makes sense to include supplier representatives as cross-functional team members. And as companies define quality as satisfying the customer, the next most logical step is to include customer representatives on cross-functional teams for quality improvement and product development.

Involving Suppliers

Once companies realized that the quality of their suppliers was inextricably linked with the quality of their products and services, they sought to involve (some might say pressure) suppliers to conform to certain quality standards. Motorola shook things up a bit when it told its six thousand suppliers that they had to apply for the Malcolm Baldrige National Quality Award if they wanted to keep doing business with Motorola. Ford, Xerox, and Florida Power and Light Company are also bringing suppliers into their quest for quality. "Common elements of these new relationships include cross-functional vendor review and development teams, which often include personnel from purchasing, quality assurance, and end-user organizations. They work so closely with suppliers that they often come to seem like a part of the suppliers' own organizations" ("Vendor Certification Improves Buyer/Seller Relationships," 1990, p. 2).

When suppliers join the cross-functional team, they have to be seen as true partners in the overall team process. The fact that a supplier has been certified or is on a "preferred" list should not be used simply to leverage a lower price. Rather, the focus should be on quality and how the suppliers' input on the team can improve the quality of the product or service. The goal should be to build a long-term relationship that leads to cost savings, improved quality, and more business for everyone.

Customer Participation

Every cross-functional team should identify its customer. The next step is to bring the customer into the team. As organizations come to see the customer as a partner and not an adversary, customers are becoming regular members of the organizations' teams. For example, systems development teams almost always include user representatives to ensure that the system meets their needs and is user-friendly. Nowadays, car manufacturers are including dealers on their cross-functional design teams to get instant feedback about how the customer likes the product instead of waiting for formal survey results. Car rental companies are involving customers on process improvement teams to solve key customer complaints. Those of us who rent cars are reaping the benefits. For example, one of the biggest complaints of car-rental customers is the time it takes them to actually get on the road after they've gotton off a plane at the airport. These customers would appreciate a company that reduces the time it takes to wait in line, to fill out the forms, to get to the car, and to get out of the parking lot. At one major rental-car company, a cross-functional team that included customers came up with a system that reduced the transaction time dramatically. By the way, as you might suspect, these changes not only result in satisfied customers but also in satisfied employees, who are dealing with fewer unhappy customers.

COLOCATION

Although we talk a great deal about how a cross-functional team functions when it comes together for meetings, much of the so-called teamwork takes place outside meetings. If we define teamwork more broadly to include all collaborative efforts, then teamwork can take place any time when at least two interdependent people get together to share information, learn, solve a problem, or make a decision. Many people still share the view that says, Only when we are face-to-face can we see eye-to-eye. If that is the case, then physical proximity can facilitate effective teamwork. And that makes sense. Although there is probably no way to accurately measure it, the opportunity to interact with your teammates on an informal, daily basis contributes to team effectiveness because it breaks down the barriers between strangers, helps overcome past relationship problems, and facilitates the growth of new partnerships. It seems clear that accessibility facilitates those hallway meetings, spontaneous get-togethers in a teammate's office, chats over coffee, meetings over lunch in the company cafeteria, and after-work sessions in a nearby restaurant. The value of colocation is only realized if it means within the same building, some would even say the same floor — in other words, a cluster of contiguous offices. "Even if you are one building away it makes a difference," says Alistair Glass, director of passive components research at AT&T Bell Laboratories in Murray Hill, New Jersey. "We have two facilities 35 miles apart and it's very clear that it's much harder [to collaborate]. Even within hallways, geography makes a difference. It's important whose lab you're next to" (Culotta, 1993, p. 22).

Once again, this is especially true for cross-functional team members with little experience in working together. When team members are permanently assigned to a cross-functional team for a specific period of time, often the organization will also decide to colocate the team members. As Joe Skraba, director of product development for Intermedics Orthopedics of Austin, Texas, put it, "We broke up the departments and put people next to each other. When you come here, you see our manufacturing engineers sitting next to our marketing people, who are sitting next to the designers" (Beckert, 1991, p. 52). It is, of course, not possible to colocate all team members when they come from different countries in addition to different functions. In those cases, the organization can move one or two of the key players or the core team to a central location for the duration of the project.

When team members are not assigned to the cross-functional team on a full-time basis, colocation is not always feasible. Often in these situations, team members belong to several cross-functional teams at the same time. It is important to recognize that these teams will not be able to take advantage of the benefits that come from colocation, such as more rapid team development, team learning, and informal problem solving. Some cross-functional teams who are not colocated try to compensate by holding off-site meetings to facilitate the development of interpersonal relationships and the building of an informal network that will encourage collaboration among team members in different locations. They may also hold the team meetings in different locations so team members get an opportunity to visit each other's work sites.

COMMUNICATIONS TECHNOLOGY

As the number of quality and teamwork initiatives increases, the number of meetings also increases. And with the increasing number of meetings, we can expect a backlash against more and more meetings. Once more we will hear, "I can't get my work done because I'm always in a meeting." This backlash will turn into a backlash against the quality and teamwork efforts. What to do? First, we need to improve the productivity of meetings using the methods described earlier in this chapter. Second, we need to carefully assess the value of face-to-face meetings for accomplishing certain goals in terms of costs versus benefits. For example, we recently calculated the cost of a client's one-hour team meeting at approximately a thousand dollars. The question for the team was, Did it get a thousand dollars in benefits from the meeting or could members have spent the time better otherwise?

There are certain team activities that seem to require a face-to-face meeting, such as developing the team vision, mission, or goals; debating strategy; or making a key decision. However, other activities can be accomplished electronically. Many organizations have wired their personal computer users into a network that allows them to communicate with team members. Every day some new software hits the market that takes advantage of these local area networks (LANs). As a result, team members can send messages, including graphics, video clips, and voice, to other members around the building or around the world. For example, members of a new-product team, simultaneously or individually, can look at an engineering drawing, test results charts or marketing data and then comment and even edit the document on-line.

Although products change quickly, there appear to be four main types of software that facilitate cross-functional teamwork (Opper, 1990):

1. *Documents Editing:* provides team members with the opportunity to edit documents on-line

2. *Managing Work-Group Communication:* facilitates team discussions, transmits messages, coordinates calendars, tracks projects, and follows up on action items

3. *Team Development:* assesses and provides feedback about team members' styles and team composition

4. *Forms Processing:* coordinates routine transactions such as forms, insurance claims, and customer complaints

In addition to reducing the number of meetings, the use of communications technology can help facilitate communication, including informal collaboration, which may be lost when team members are not colocated. As teams become increasingly both cross-functional and international, technology will be used extensively as a substitute for team meetings.

Video Teleconferencing

Although many companies are using teleconferencing for cross-functional team meetings, the results are, at best, mixed. While it does save travel time and expenses, it does not eliminate team meetings. In most cases, some team members are in a company meeting room in one location while others are in a similar room in another location. The technology usually allows team members to view the same documents in both rooms on the video screen. The medium received a big push during the Gulf War, when all business travel was severely restricted. Many companies used video conferencing during that time. However, many of the limitations of the technology also became more apparent. For example, it is often difficult to hear comments from anyone but the few people seated near the head table. It is also hard to see everyone. In general, the discussions lack an easy, informal flow.

However, despite the drawbacks, video conferencing will be necessary in the future as cross-functional teams become more international. As a result, more will be invested to make the technology more user-friendly and to train team members to make better use of it.

THE IMPORTANCE OF INTERNAL TEAM DYNAMICS

Group dynamics has always been an important ingredient in the success of a team. However, as the new organizations create more horizontal team structures, internal dynamics will have a different focus. Teams will need adaptable members and flexible leaders, who can value and incorporate the contributions of people from different functions and cultures to gain a competitive advantage. Teams will need to get better at quickly establishing trust, creating open communication, resolving conflicts, and making better use of meeting time as well as communications technology.

While all these internal team factors are necessary, they are not sufficient for sustaining effective cross-functional teamwork. The leadership of the organization must work to create a culture that encourages and supports cross-functional collaboration. Chapter Thirteen provides specific advice for senior-level managers who are serious about creating a team-based organization.

PART THREE

Toward
Cross-Functional
Teams

CHAPTER

13

Management's Role in Building the Team-Based Organization

Look around at the most successful organizations today—you'll find quality at the core of their corporate goals and teamwork as the principal strategy for achieving those goals. As with most paradigm shifts, we rarely recognize the change while we are living through it; as a result, we fail to successfully manage the transition. The purpose of this chapter is to suggest some ways to create an organization that has quality as its goal and cross-functional teamwork as its strategy.

A quiet movement is working its way across organizations as cross-functional teams are being formed to meet the demands of customers for better quality and service.

Note: This chapter draws heavily on my article "Getting Into Shape," *Managing Service Quality*, July 1992, pp. 251–254.

- Insurance companies are organizing their policyholder-services employees into multiskilled teams, which are better able to service all customers in a region or line of business.

- In the pharmaceutical industry, account management teams have been formed around major customers, re-placing a product-driven strategy with a customer-focused strategy.

- In highly competitive service industries such as hotels and rental cars, teams of front-line service workers are being teamed with customers to come up with solutions to some of the customers' biggest problems.

- Consulting firms are reorganizing their staff experts into permanent multidisciplinary teams aligned with their major customers or client groups.

THE CHALLENGE

Since we seem to have accepted teamwork as a necessary strategy for success, the challenge now is to make it work. Typically, the response is to give everyone some training in teamwork skills. While I believe training is important and necessary, it is not sufficient to make the successful shift to a team-based organization. Unfortunately, the emphasis on training detracts from focusing on the other critical aspects of organization change. We already know how to train employees in team effectiveness, yet we keep trying to perfect team training techniques. In a recent major examination of work teams in America, Wilson Learning Corporation found that almost 80 percent of the respondents named organizational barriers (including the entire infrastructure) as the major road-block to effective teamwork (Leimbach, 1992).

Since we already know how to teach people to use the consensus method in team decision making, why do we keep developing more survival exercises? We have been lost on the moon, in the desert, at sea, and in at least a dozen other places. Do we still need more? We already have many five-, six-, and seven-step problem-solving models for teams. Why are we spending time developing variations on these models? There are several very fine assessment tools for measuring team effectiveness. Do we really need another one? My point is obvious: We seem to be spending more time doing what we already do well—training and developing teams—when we should be turning our attention to organizations struggling with the challenge of embedding teamwork into their organizational fiber.

WHAT MANAGEMENT CAN DO

Talk the Talk

The leaders of organizations that want to succeed as team-based organizations must continually say the right words. The leadership must send out a clear and consistent message that cross-functional teamwork is its strategy for achieving world-class quality. This message must appear in all written presentations. If you do not have a vision, values, or mission statement, the first step is to create one in concert with the leadership team. The vision should be a statement of your "desired" or "preferred" future as opposed to your predicted future. A vision is more than an idea—it is a force, a picture that provides a future focus for the organization. Or as one of my clients put it simply, "It's where we want to be."

Here are the vision statements regarding teamwork of several organizations:

- Quality is our first priority and teamwork is our standard in all aspects of what we do.

- Our goal is to establish a climate of openness, mutual respect, and teamwork.

- We seek teamwork throughout the organization... participative goal setting...and decision making at the lowest level.

With a clear message in hand, the organization's leadership should use every opportunity to pound it home. At every company seminar, leadership meeting, awards dinner, or other similar occasion, the cross-functional teamwork charge should be sounded. Company publications should also be used to promote the theme of teamwork. Stories in the annual report, status reports, in-house newspapers, and newsletters as well as corporate magazines should regularly carry stories of the benefits of teamwork and the valuable contributions of team players. Repetition is important because employees are used to corporate themes that change quickly, often referred to as the "topic du jour" or the "flavor of the month." As a result, employees take the cynical view that if they do nothing and just wait, a new "priority" will emerge to replace the current fad.

I work with managers who ask impatiently, "How many times do I have to make my teamwork speech?" And I always reply, "As often as possible and as many times as I ask you."

Walk the Talk

To those cynics who say talk is cheap, I say you are correct but it is where we start. But although it is important to say the right words, it is not enough. The members of the leadership team must also live by the words. They must act and work like a team. They must be a model of cross-functional teamwork that the rest of the organization looks to for guidance. It is by now an axiom that the most powerful motivator of employee behavior is the behavior of the boss. Most top management teams and many middle management teams are cross-functional. As a result, they are in a perfect position to demonstrate the value of cross-functional teamwork that sends a powerful message to others in the organization.

On my first visit to the offices of a new client, I noticed

that there was a framed copy of the vision statement in every office and conference room. I remarked that this was an impressive display of the importance of the statement. To which my client contact responded, "And the CEO measures every decision for its consistency with the vision." Later, I wondered how he, as a midlevel manager, was so sure of this, since he rarely interacted with the CEO. The point: He probably did not know it for sure, but he believed it! And you can be sure he checked every one of his actions for their support of the company's vision.

One of my current clients is trying to install teamwork as a strategy in the organization. It's been decided that we should conduct a course in teamwork for everyone. Significantly, the first to be trained are the vice president and her direct reports, which sends the message to the rest of the organization that this training is important for everyone from the top to the bottom. Incidentally, a key unit of the course for the top team is what they can do personally and as a team to create a team-based culture.

By contrast, some years ago in another organization, I was conducting a team-building course for a director-level group. When I would urge them to work together across department lines, they would respond, "You better tell our bosses first." They went on to tell horror stories of directives from their superiors not to work with this group, to hold up work needed by another, or to withhold information from someone else. The message was clear: We talk cross-functional teamwork but we don't live it.

Recognize and Reward

We start with the basic premise that people will exhibit the behaviors that are rewarded and recognized. An organization's formal awards program should give awards to teams. In addition, the criteria for individual awards should include team player behaviors. Since Chapter Nine includes a detailed description of a number of awards programs for cross-functional teamwork, our purpose here is simply to underscore the need for management to get behind efforts to create and manage formal and informal efforts to recognize successful cross-functional teamwork.

Many firms are moving to awards that go only to teams — that is, no one wins unless the team wins. This type of awards program encourages people to pitch in and help the team succeed. The key to a successful team awards program begins with allowing team members to select their own rewards as long as they stay within a budgetary limit, which explains the popularity of catalogue programs. While everyone says they want money as a reward, studies continually show that employees want recognition for their contribution to the company. Noncash rewards provide recognition from management and peers. Perhaps more important, the recognition factor lasts long after the money has been spent. In one company I work with, which provides cash awards, people also receive a plaque, which serves as a permanent reminder of their success. One final but significant factor in team awards is the selection process. I strongly recommend a peer review process that is controlled by nonmanagement employees. *Peer review* means that employees develop the criteria, review the awards proposals, make the decisions, and present the awards. One company includes several management people on the committee to ensure organizational perspective. It also rotates committee membership so that all employees learn how the program works in practice.

Focus on Performance

It is important that the performance appraisal, compensation, and promotion policies of an organization support the goal of teamwork as a business strategy. I believe we should begin with the appraisal process, because it is a regularly scheduled activity that tells employees how their performance measures up. Therefore, it is extremely important that team player behaviors be included prominently among the factors that are rated. Many companies are already including team characteristics in their appraisal forms. Here are some examples from forms I have collected (see Chapter Nine for a more in-depth discussion of performance appraisal):

- Understands and supports the goals of the team.
- Consults with others and shares information.
- Negotiates differences effectively.
- Constructively challenges prevailing points of view.
- Open to unsolicited ideas and opinions.
- Friendly and approachable in working with others.

Promotion is a specific and visible reward for performance. It is both a way to reward team players and to send a message to others in the organization that teamwork is the goal and team players are valued. As one manager said to me, "We promote team players and we make it clear that profit-goal achievement alone will not lead to a promotion." However, to be really effective, the promotion must be made public in a substantive manner. The reasons for the promotion must be made clear and specific. When a person is promoted because he or she is both technically competent and an effective team player, the accomplishments in both areas should be highlighted. A carefully worded promotional announcement makes it clear that getting ahead in the organization requires a combination of technical and teamwork skills. Here is an example of a short announcement:

Donna Jamieson
Promoted to Project Director

Donna Jamieson has been promoted to project director in recognition of her creativity as a systems developer on PBAT, YAMS, and ORRIS. She continues to develop her technical skills via in-company workshops and external seminars and she recently completed course requirements for an M.S. degree in computer science from S.U. As co-chair of the user interface teams and a member of the BIRKS Task Force, Donna has shown herself to be

someone who can be depended upon to do her homework, to pitch in when other people need help, and make
sure everyone gets a chance to participate in team decisions. She is honest, ethical, and willing to speak her mind
on important organizational issues. Donna contributes
technical excellence as well as positive team spirit to our
organization [Parker, 1990, p. 139].

Be a Storyteller

It is important that the organization develop a culture that
values teamwork and team players. Any organizational culture
is composed of a series of norms, stories, and myths that
enhance and shape the behavior of employees. All these cultural manifestations are part of the informal systems of the
organization. Stories give people a flavor of the company—
they tell people what type of behavior is valued. When these
stories are told and retold and subsequently embellished, they
become myths and the people in the stories become legends.
Ultimately, the values in the stories may translate into specific
behavioral expectations, which we call norms. Norms are simply the day-to-day informal guidelines that tell employees what
behavior is acceptable.

For example, in the course of an organizational diagnosis,
I was told, "You should have been there when Deborah told
the vice president his marketing plan was all wet." This was an
organizational story that was enhanced to the point of being a
myth. In fact, Deborah did not say the plan was "all wet." She
just suggested some alternatives that were, in turn, accepted
by the vice president. The point was that no one had ever had
the courage to challenge the ideas of an upper-management
person; it served to establish a new team player norm, that
disagreement is acceptable.

What do you make of this next myth about a legendary
figure in the history of the company? "He once drove through
a blinding snowstorm to make a delivery to a customer." On
the surface, this looks like a story about obsessive commitment
to serve the customer. While it is clearly a service story, it also
promotes individual heroics, rather than team success. It tells

people that if you want to get ahead, look for opportunities to stand out from the crowd.

On the other hand, another story in a similar vein seems to promote the values of team play over individual effort. In this example, a cross-functional new-product team composed of highly educated professionals worked all night loading trucks with product to meet a test-market deadline. People in the company enjoyed telling the story of these well-dressed MBAs who got their hands dirty doing what was necessary to meet their team objective.

Understanding the importance of positive myth encourages leaders to use every opportunity to tell and retell stories that laud cross-functional teamwork. These stories have the effect of making the vision and values statements come alive for people in the organization. They put life into the words and meaning into the actions of the company's heroes and heroines. Ultimately, the stories get folded into the daily life of the organization and eventually become the norms that shape and guide teamwork behavior.

Provide Resources

Teams cannot swim alone. They need resources to survive and thrive. Resources can mean many things.

Space.   There is no substitute for good, well-equipped meeting rooms. Let's face it, as much as we hate meetings, teams do much of their work in meetings. The rooms should have good, basic meeting-room equipment such as flip charts or whiteboards, overhead projectors, and video tape players. In addition, the allocation of the space should be well managed. In one organization, unfortunately, the administration of the meeting rooms is so ineffective that many teams have given up and simply use tables in the company cafeteria.

Technology.   There are many new methods of electronic communication available today that can enhance the effectiveness of teams. Many of these methods can improve communication and often decrease a team's dependence on face-to-face meetings. Electronic mail, local area networks, voice mail, faxing, conference calls, teleconferencing, and video teleconferencing are different methods of team communication that increase the effectiveness of a team.

Training.   We end where we began. While training alone will not change an organizational culture, it can support and facilitate the change process. Training can do two important things to help create a team-based organization. First, training provides people with the skills and knowledge to help them be successful. Second, it sends a message that teamwork is important; in fact, so important that we are investing in programs to upgrade team effectiveness.

   Several types of training are necessary. People need to learn how to be a team player, teams need to learn what constitutes an effective cross-functional team, and team leaders need to learn basic leadership skills, such as planning and facilitating meetings, decision making, problem solving, resolving conflict, and communicating. (See Chapter Ten for a detailed description of team-learning activities.)

CREATING SUCCESSFUL CROSS-FUNCTIONAL TEAMWORK

We begin with the fundamental premise that teams are a critical factor in a successful business strategy. While it is important to acknowledge the central role of cross-functional teams, it is not enough to simply set up teams, provide training, and hope for the best. As my colleague, team-building consultant Jim Shonk, says, "Where organizations see teams as a way of addressing critical business issues, they find time for and support teamwork. Sometimes organizations have to be in crisis before they perceive a need to do something different.

To be hoped is that more and more organizations will ask, 'how can we get better?'" (Shonk, 1992, p. 156).

Successful implementation of a team-based strategy requires a commitment to say the right words—that is, that teamwork and team players are critical to success—and to drive that message home as often as possible. In tandem with the words must come the actions demonstrating that the organization's leadership is a living example of successful cross-functional teamwork.

Successful cross-functional teams and team players must be rewarded for their support of the organization's vision and values. Related to rewards is inclusion of team player behaviors in the company's performance appraisal system. Both team-oriented awards and performance appraisals are tangible and visible support for teamwork as the vehicle for implementation of the corporate strategy.

In addition, the leaders of the organization must work to create a team-based culture by telling organizational stories that perpetuate the heroes and heroines of teamwork. As these stories become embedded in the fabric of the organization, they translate into the daily norms that shape employee behavior in support of team play.

And finally, teams need resources of all types to increase their chances of success and as another bit of evidence that the organization is committed to teamwork as a serious business strategy. The Wilson Learning Corporation's study of teamwork concluded that the successful team-based organization "is one in which top management is strongly committed to breaking down barriers, eliminating, where possible, internal competition for resources, and avoiding the singling out of individuals for personal recognition and achievement. The . . . organization also provides a performance appraisal and compensation process that promotes interdependent achievement, but with individual accountability. The organization focuses not so much on individual achievement, but on individual contributions to group achievement" (Leimbach, 1992, p. 16).

C H A P T E R

14

Jump-Starting the Change to Cross-Functional Teams

OK, you're convinced. Cross-functional teams can be a powerful vehicle for increasing the effectiveness of your organization. You want to start using these teams to streamline the product development cycle, improve the quality of your products and services, increase customer satisfaction, or reorganize the business. You want to know where to start. Or, your organization is littered with teams of all types and degrees of success. You are looking for ways to improve the functioning of the existing teams.

AS A TOP MANAGER

Teamwork begins at home. First, look at your own team. It is probably a cross-functional group rather than a team. Begin by making sure your team has a clear set of performance objectives (not just the company's or division's objectives) and must produce joint output (output that requires the collaboration of team members). Ask for feedback on whether your team is perceived as an effective team. In other words, whether you are seen as a model of cross-functional teamwork, to be emulated.

Second, think about the teamwork message you are sending to the organization. Are people clear that you value cross-functional teamwork? Will team members be rewarded or at least acknowledged for collaboration with their colleagues from other departments? Do teams receive the resources they need to support their efforts? If you have some questions about what you can do, turn back to Chapter Thirteen.

AS A TEAM LEADER

As a leader of a cross-functional team, you are probably aware of the potential of the diverse group of colleagues and strangers on the team. If you want to take advantage of that potential, start by carefully assessing the team's strengths and weaknesses. Begin with the Survey of Cross-Functional Teamwork at the end of the book. How does your team stack up? Ask other team members to do their own assessment. In fact, get the whole team involved in the evaluation and then the development of an improvement plan. When you have identified some areas for improvement, refer to the appropriate chapters in the book for ideas on what to do next.

AS A MIDLEVEL MANAGER

Let's assume a number of your people serve on cross-functional teams. The challenges here are great for you. You must balance the need to achieve your department objectives with the need to provide support for the team's objectives. One way to do this is to talk with the leaders of cross-functional teams and with your people who serve on these teams. In these meetings, clarify the best ways to meet team and department needs and establish some norms for regular communication, including input from the team leader for use in performance appraisal.

AS A HUMAN RESOURCE PROFESSIONAL

You can look for ways to provide support for leaders and members of cross-functional teams as well as for the functional department managers. Training for leaders and members will be critical, and you can facilitate the team learning process (Chapter Ten can help here). At some point, team leaders and others will come to you for ideas on how to reward cross-functional teamwork. Get a jump on those questions by reviewing Chapter Nine.

No matter who you are or where you are in the organization, never lose your sense of humor. The diversity of cross-functional teams will produce some conflicts, some strange and strained relationships, and some tense moments. But working with allies, enemies, and other strangers will also give you some wonderful and funny moments. Take the time to enjoy them.

Tools for Developing Cross-Functional Teams

The tools on the pages that follow are designed to supplement the ideas presented in this book.

A. Experiences in Teamwork

These cases are used in team-training sessions for cross-functional teams. When you discuss and analyze the cases, first identify the issues highlighted in each. By *issues*, I mean such things as empowerment, leadership, team dynamics, and goals. Refer to the chapters in the book that focus on the pertinent issues as you discuss possible ways to deal with the situation.

B. Survey of Cross-Functional Teamwork: An Evaluation Tool

This survey is designed to help you assess your team and plan to increase its effectiveness. When you have identified areas for improvement, you can refer to the chapters in the book appropriate to your action plan. (For information on how to obtain copies of the Survey of Cross-Functional Teamwork, contact Glenn M. Parker Associates, 41 Woodlane Road, Lawrenceville, NJ 08648.)

C. Read Any Good Books Lately?
An Annotated Reading List

Here I offer an annotated list of the most useful books on teamwork.

D. Parker's Top Ten Ways to Ensure Team Failure

Just in case you didn't get the message, here's one final reminder. Have fun!

A

Experiences
in Teamwork

Directions: Please read each case and (1) identify the teamwork issue and (2) decide what should be done to address the situation.

1. A member of your quality action team is not pulling his weight. His work is consistently late and of poor quality. Other team members either have to work late to include his section in the final report or revise the section to bring it up to the standards of the remainder of the document. He works for a director in another department.

2. You are the leader of a development team. Your team has completed a careful assessment of the market potential of a new product and has prepared a detailed action plan. At this point, your boss strongly suggests that the direction and focus of the team change.

3. You are a member of a systems development team. You and several other team members feel the meetings are a

boring succession of technical reports with no opportunity for relationship building. When you raise the issue with the team leader, she indicates that other members seem to like the meetings because they start and end on time and they stick to the agenda.

4. You have agreed to conduct a critical meeting next week of your cross-functional team with one of your major clients. However, your department director just asked you to handle a problem with another customer, which means you will not have adequate time to prepare for the client meeting. Other team members cannot handle the meeting for you because they do not have the necessary background.

B

Survey of Cross-Functional Teams: An Evaluation Tool

This survey includes a series of factors that contribute to the success of cross-functional teams. Please review the list and (1) indicate the extent to which you believe each factor is important to the success of your cross-functional team and (2) assess your team in each of the areas.

Success Factors.

Factor	Importance					Assessment					Comments
	Unimportant	Somewhat Important	Important	Very Important	Critical	Strongly Disagree	Disagree	Neutral	Agree	Strongly Agree	
1. **Leadership** The leader has the necessary team management skills.	1	2	3	4	5	1	2	3	4	5	
2. **Authority** The authority is clear and consistent with the team's responsibility.	1	2	3	4	5	1	2	3	4	5	
3. **Goals** The team has a clear set of goals.	1	2	3	4	5	1	2	3	4	5	
4. **Decision Making** Team members have a real opportunity to participate in key team decisions.	1	2	3	4	5	1	2	3	4	5	
5. **Recognition** Individual members receive appropriate recognition for their contributions to team effort.	1	2	3	4	5	1	2	3	4	5	

6. Roles
Members are clear about what is expected of them.

1 2 3 4 5   1 2 3 4 5

7. Boundary Management
The team does a good job of developing relationships with key stakeholders in other parts of the organization.

1 2 3 4 5   1 2 3 4 5

8. Performance Appraisal
Performance on the cross-functional team is included in each member's performance appraisal.

1 2 3 4 5   1 2 3 4 5

9. Team Training
Leaders and members have been trained in team effectiveness skills.

1 2 3 4 5   1 2 3 4 5

10. Team Meetings
Meetings are well planned and executed.

1 2 3 4 5   1 2 3 4 5

11. Communications Technologies
The team makes effective use of nonmeeting methods (e.g., LANs) to communicate information.

1 2 3 4 5   1 2 3 4 5

Success Factors, Cont'd.

Factor	Importance					Assessment					Comments
	Unimportant	Somewhat Important	Important	Very Important	Critical	Strongly Disagree	Disagree	Neutral	Agree	Strongly Agree	
12. Team Size The team is small enough to ensure effective communication and decision making.	1	2	3	4	5	1	2	3	4	5	
13. Management Support Management actively supports the work of the team.	1	2	3	4	5	1	2	3	4	5	
14. Colocation All key team members work in the same location.	1	2	3	4	5	1	2	3	4	5	
15. Customers and Suppliers As appropriate, customer and supplier representatives are included.	1	2	3	4	5	1	2	3	4	5	

16. Cross-Training
Members receive technical training in other team disciplines and functions.

1 2 3 4 5   1 2 3 4 5

17. Openness
Members feel free to express their views on key issues.

1 2 3 4 5   1 2 3 4 5

18. Conflict Resolution
Differences are resolved openly and constructively.

1 2 3 4 5   1 2 3 4 5

19. Cultural and Style Differences
The team appreciates and utilizes the different styles represented on the team.

1 2 3 4 5   1 2 3 4 5

20. Client Focus
The team's primary emphasis is on satisfying the client's needs.

1 2 3 4 5   1 2 3 4 5

In general, our cross-functional team is successful

1 Strongly Disagree   2 Disagree   3 Neutral   4 Agree   5 Strongly Agree

Survey of Cross-Functional Teamwork
Analyzing the Results.

Strengths   = High Importance (3, 4, 5)
                      High Assessment (4, 5)

Improvement   = High Importance (3, 4, 5)
Opportunity   Low Assessment (1, 2)

1. What are the strengths of your team?

2. What are your improvement opportunities?

■ Which factors does the team control?

■ Which factors can the team influence?

■ Which factors are clearly beyond the team's control or ability
   to influence?

**Survey of Cross-Functional Teamwork
Developing an Action Plan.**

---

1. How can you build on your strengths?

2. How will you address your improvement opportunities?

Read Any Good Books Lately? An Annotated Reading List

I am very often asked, "If we want to start a library of books on teamwork, which ones would you recommend (besides yours, of course)?" With the boom in teamwork as a business strategy and its relationship to quality, there have been a load of new books out in the past few years. Some focus on specific aspects of teamwork, such as self-directed teams; some concentrate on teams in the quality process; a few are directed at managers; and still others focus on facilitators.

With that in mind, what follows is my short list of books to start a team library.

Note: An earlier version of this list appeared in my Leadership Insights column in *Today's Team Facilitator*, August 1993, p. 8, published by Wentworth Publishing, Lancaster, Pennsylvania.

FOR FACILITATORS

The classic in the field is a little book called *Team Building: Issues and Alternatives* by William Dyer (Addison-Wesley, 1977). It is chock-full of sensible ideas, easy-to-understand concepts, and some practical exercises and activities in such areas as starting a new team, resolving team member conflict, revitalizing a complacent team, and reducing interteam conflict.

A much bigger and more expensive book, actually a manual, is *The Team Building Sourcebook* by Steven Phillips and Robin Elledge (University Associates, 1989). It contains many sample questionnaires, training designs, checklists, and exercises for every step in the team-building process. A very nice feature is the ability to reproduce the pages without violating the copyright.

FOR MANAGERS

Two recent books will help managers understand how to create a team environment and how they can support the process. My colleague James Shonk's book is a brief but tightly focused set of directives covering types of teams, team training, team leadership, and most important, deciding whether teams are right for your organization. The book is called *Team-Based Organizations* (Business One Irwin, 1992).

The Wisdom of Teams (Harvard Business School Press, 1993) is a major book by two McKinsey and Company consultants, who report on a study of more than fifty teams in thirty different companies. Jon Katzenbach and Douglas Smith tell us that successful teams result from a demanding performance challenge or goal. Again and again, the authors point to the need for a clear purpose, specific goals, a plan of attack, and a sense of accountability.

FOR SELF-DIRECTED TEAMS

I recommend two big books and one manual. The big books are from two big consulting firms. Development Dimensions International principals Richard Wellins, William Byham, and Jeanne Wilson have produced *Empowered Teams* (Jossey-Bass, 1991), a good book for starting the process. Leaders of Zenger-Miller, Linda Moran, Ed Musselwhite, and John Zenger have joined with Jack Orsburn to produce another good basic book, *Self-Directed Work Teams* (Business One Irwin, 1990).

Richard Kropp and I recently produced a manual of practical exercises called *50 Activities for Self-Directed Teams* (HRD Press, 1994).

IN GENERAL

The Superteam Solution by Colin Hastings, Peter Bixby, and Rani Chaudhry-Lawton (University Associates, 1987) is full of insights and practical suggestions not found in other books in the field. The authors are from England and they provide a different perspective on teams.

A good book of readings is *Team Building: Blueprints for Productivity and Satisfaction* (University Associates, 1987), edited by Brendan Reddy and Kaleel Jamison. It includes nineteen chapters written by different authors on a variety of topics, including some not dealt with elsewhere, such as teams in voluntary organizations and government agencies as well as multicultural and multifunctional teams.

ABOUT EMPOWERMENT

By now, just about everyone owns a copy of Peter Block's *The Empowered Manager* (Jossey-Bass, 1987), but of more use to practitioners may be *Empowerment in Organizations* (University Associates, 1990) by Judith Vogt and Kenneth Murrell. It contains lots of practical tools, lists, and ideas for implementing empowerment.

FOR LEADERS

The best book, bar none, is *Leaders: The Strategies for Taking Charge* (HarperCollins, 1985) by Warren Bennis and Burt Nanus. The authors interviewed eighty leaders of a variety of organizations and isolated their distinguishing characteristics.

ON GOAL SETTING

An excellent little book full of wonderful insights and practical tips is *Goal Setting: A Motivational Technique That Works* (Prentice-Hall, 1984) by Edwin Locke and Gary Latham.

TO REWARD TEAMS AND TEAM PLAYERS

There are two big studies: *People, Performance and Pay* (American Compensation Association, 1987) by Carla O'Dell and Jerry McAdams and *Capitalizing on Human Assets* (American Quality and Productivity Center and American Compensation Association, 1992) by Jerry McAdams and Elizabeth Hawk.

PUTTING IT ALL IN PERSPECTIVE

Take a look at Charles Handy's *The Age of Unreason* (Harvard Business School Press, 1990) for a view of the future of organizations by a friendly British observer.

D

Parker's Top Ten Ways to Ensure Team Failure

What is so magical about lists of ten? We have the Ten Commandments and the ten best movies of the year. And, of course, David Letterman's many top ten lists. Now we have my list of ten — the top ten ways to ensure that teams will fail in your organization. So, with tongue firmly planted in cheek, here goes:

10. Don't listen to any new idea or recommendation from a team. It's probably not a good idea since it is new and comes from a team.

Note: This list originally appeared in my Leadership Insights column in *Today's Team Facilitator*, September 1993, p. 8, published by Wentworth Publishing, Lancaster, Pennsylvania.

9. Don't give teams any additional resources to help solve problems in their area. Teams are supposed to save money and make do with less. Besides, they will probably just waste more time and money.

8. Treat all problems as signs of failure and treat all failures as a reason to disband teams and downgrade team members. Teams are supposed to make things better, not cause you more problems.

7. Create a system that requires lots of reviews and signatures to get approvals for all changes, purchases, and new procedures. You can't be too careful these days.

6. Get the security department involved to make it difficult for teams to get information about the business. Don't let those team members near any computers. You don't want them finding out how the business is run.

5. Assign a manager to keep an eye on teams in your area. Tell the teams that he or she is there to help *facilitate* (teams like that word)—but what you really want these managers to do is control the direction of the teams and report back to you on any deviations from your plan.

4. When you reorganize or change policies and procedures, do not involve team members in the decision or give them any advance warning. This will just slow things down and make it difficult to implement the changes.

3. Cut out all training of team members. Problem solving is just common sense anyway, and besides, all that training really accomplishes is to make a few consultants really rich.

2. Express your criticisms freely and withhold your praise and recognition. Teams need to know where they have screwed up so that they can change. If you give out praise, people will expect a raise or a reward, and you don't want that.

1. Above all, remember you know best. That's why they pay you the big bucks. Never let team members forget that.

REFERENCES

Allaire, P. A. *Xerox 2000: Putting It Together.* Stamford, Conn.: Xerox Corporate Communications, Feb. 1992.

Ancona, D. G., and Caldwell, D. "Beyond Boundary Spanning: Managing External Dependence in Product Development Teams." *Journal of High Technology Management Research,* 1990a, *1*(2), 119–135.

Ancona, D. G., and Caldwell, D. "Improving the Performance of New Product Teams." *Research-Technology Management,* Mar.-Apr., 1990b, pp. 25–29.

Ancona, D. G., and Caldwell, D. "Cross-Functional Teams: Blessing or Curse for New Product Development." *MIT Management,* Spring 1991, pp. 11–16.

Ancona, D. G., and Caldwell, D. "Speeding Product Development: Making Teamwork Work." Cambridge, Mass.: Sloan School of Management, July 1992.

Anderson, C. "Curing What Ails U.S. Health Care." *Quality Progress,* Apr. 1992, pp. 35–38.

Austin, N. K. "Updating the Performance Review." *Working Woman,* Nov. 1992, pp. 32–35.

Beckert, B. A. "Changing the Culture." *Computer-Aided Engineering,* Oct. 1991, pp. 51–56.

Belasco, J. A. "Empowerment as a Business Strategy." *Executive Excellence,* June 1991, pp. 15–17.

Bennis, W. G., and Nanus, B. *Leaders: The Strategies for Taking Charge.* New York: HarperCollins, 1985.

Bennis, W. G., and Slater, P. *The Temporary Society.* New York: HarperCollins, 1968.

Block, P. *The Empowered Manager: Positive Political Skills at Work.* San Francisco: Jossey-Bass, 1987.

Bouchard, T. J., Draden, G., and Barasaloux, J. "Brainstorming Procedure, Group Size and Sex as Determinants of the Problem Solving Effectiveness of Groups and Individuals." *Journal of Applied Psychology,* 1974, 59(2), 135–138.

Bouchard, T. J., and Hare, M. "Size, Performance and Potential in Brainstorming Groups." *Journal of Applied Psychology,* 1970, 54(2), 51–55.

Clark, K. B., and Wheelwright, S. C. "Organizing and Leading 'Heavyweight' Development Teams." *California Management Review,* Spring 1992, pp. 9–28.

Cleland-Hamnett, W., and Retzer, J. "Crossing Agency Boundaries." *Environmental Forum,* Mar.-Apr. 1993, pp. 17–21.

Combs, G., and Gomez-Meija, L. R. "Cross-Functional Pay Strategies in High Technology Firms." *Compensation and Benefits Review,* Sept.-Oct. 1991, pp. 40–48.

Culotta, E. "Teamwork Is Key to Solving Complex Research Problems." *Scientist,* Mar. 8, 1993, pp. 20–22.

Davis, S. M., and Lawrence, P. *Matrix.* Reading, Mass.: Addison-Wesley, 1977.

Deming, W. E. "The Merit System: The Annual Appraisal: Destroyer of People." Paper presented at A Day with Dr. W. Edward Deming, University of Michigan, 1987.

Doherty, E. M., Nord, W. R., and McAdams, J. L. "Gainsharing and Organization Development: A Productive Strategy." *Journal of Applied Behavioral Science,* 1989, 25(3), 209–229.

Dowler, T. *SBDM: Another Look at School-Based Decision-Making.* Frankfort, Ky.: Kentucky Education Association, 1991.

Dowst, S., and Raia, E. "Design '88: Teaming Up." *Purchasing,* Mar. 10, 1988, pp. 80–91.

Doyle, M. F. "Cross-Functional Implementation Teams." *Purchasing World,* Feb. 1991, pp. 20–21.

Doyle, M., and Strauss, D. *How to Make Meetings Work.* Chicago: Playboy Press, 1976.

Dumaine, B. "How Managers Can Succeed Through Speed." *Fortune,* Feb. 13, 1989, pp. 54–59.

Dumaine, B. "The Bureaucracy Busters." *Fortune,* June 17, 1991, pp. 35–50.

Dyer, W. G. *Team Building: Issues and Alternatives.* Reading, Mass.: Addison-Wesley, 1977.

Edwards, M. R. "Making Performance Appraisal Meaningful and Fair." *Business,* July-Sept. 1989, pp. 17–25.

Edwards, M. R. "Accurate Performance Measurement Tools." *HR Magazine,* June 1991, pp. 95–98.

Eisman, R. "The Rewards of Teamwork." *Incentive,* Feb. 1990, pp. 52–55.

Elliott, V. "Motivating Bank Employees to Think Like Business Owners." *Bankers Magazine,* May-June 1991, pp. 70–74.

Fern, E. F. "The Use of Focus Groups for Idea Generation." *Journal of Marketing Research,* 1982, *19,* 1–13.

Fried, L. "Team Size and Productivity in Systems Development." *Journal of Information Systems Management,* Summer 1991, pp. 27–35.

Gordon, J. "Work Teams: How Far Have They Come?" *Training,* Oct. 1992, pp. 59–64.

Hackman, J. R., and Vidmar, N. "Effects of Size and Task Type on Group Performance and Member Reactions." *Sociomet,* 1970, *33,* 37–54.

Halverson, C. B. "Managing Differences on Muticultural Teams." *Cultural Diversity at Work,* May 1992, pp. 10–11.

Handy, C. *The Age of Unreason.* Boston: Harvard Business School Press, 1990.

Hastings, C., Bixby, P., and Chaudhry-Lawton, R. *The Superteam Solution*. San Diego, Calif.: University Associates, 1987.

Henkoff, R. "Making Your Office More Productive." *Fortune*, Feb. 25, 1991a, pp. 72–84.

Henkoff, R. "For States: Reform Turns Radical." *Fortune*, Oct. 21, 1991b, pp. 137–139.

Hill, C. H., and Yamada, K. "Motorola Illustrates How an Aged Giant Can Remain Vibrant." *Wall Street Journal*, Dec. 9, 1992, pp. A1, A18.

Hills, C. H. "Making the Team." *Sales and Marketing Management*, Feb. 1992, pp. 54–57.

Hoerr, J. "Benefits for the Back Office, Too." *Business Week*, July 10, 1989, p. 59.

Huret, J. "Paying for Team Results." *HR Magazine*, May 1991, pp. 39–41.

Johnson, R. "Milacron Survives in Dog-Eat-Dog Industry by Forming Wolfpack." *Total Quality*, Sept. 1992, p. 6.

Kaeter, M. "Cross-Training: The Tactical View." *Training*, Mar. 1993, pp. 40–46.

Kanin-Lovers, J. "Motivating the New Work Force." *Journal of Compensation and Benefits*, Sept.-Oct. 1990, pp. 50–52.

Katzenbach, J. R., and Smith, D. K. "The Discipline of Teams." *Harvard Business Review*, Mar.-Apr. 1993a, pp. 111–120.

Katzenbach, J. R., and Smith, D. K. *The Wisdom of Teams*. Boston: Harvard Business School Press, 1993b.

Kieffer, G. D. *The Strategy of Meetings*. New York: Simon & Schuster, 1988.

Kohn, A. *No Contest*. Boston: Houghton Mifflin, 1986.

Kull, D. "Software Development: The Consensus Approach." *Computer and Communications Decisions*, Aug. 1987, pp. 63–69.

Kumar, S., and Gupta, Y. P. "Cross-Functional Teams Improve Manufacturing at Motorola's Austin Plant." *Industrial Engineering*, May 1991, pp. 32–36.

Larson, C. "Team Tactics Can Cut Product Development Costs." *Journal of Business Strategy*, Sept.-Oct. 1988, pp. 22–25.

Lawler, E. E., III. *High-Involvement Management: Participative Strategies for Improving Organizational Performance.* San Francisco: Jossey-Bass, 1986.

Lawler, E. E., III. "Gainsharing Theory and Research: Findings and Future Directions." In W. A. Pasmore and R. W. Woodman (eds.), *Research in Organizational Change and Development.* Greenwich, Conn.: JAI Press, 1988.

Lawrence, P. R., and Lorsch, J. W. *Organization and Environment: Managing Differentiation and Integration.* Boston: Harvard Business School, 1967.

Leavitt, D. "Team Techniques in System Development." *Datamation,* Nov. 15, 1987, pp. 78–86.

Leimbach, M. P. *Meeting the Competitive Challenge.* Eden Prairie, Minn.: Wilson Learning Corporation, 1992.

Lewis, A. C., Sadosky, T. L., and Connolly, T. C. "The Effectiveness of Group Brainstorming in Engineering Problem Solving." *IEEE Transactions in Engineering Management,* 1975, 22, 119–124.

Lewis, M. *Liar's Poker.* New York: Penguin, 1989.

Locke, E. A., and Latham, G. P. *Goal Setting: A Motivational Technique That Works!* Englewood Cliffs, N.J.: Prentice-Hall, 1984.

Loehr, L. "Between Silence and Voice: Communicating in Cross-Functional Project Teams." *IEEE Transactions on Professional Communication,* Mar. 1991, 34(1), 51–56.

Lyons, T. F., Krachenberg, A. R., and Henke, J. W. "Mixed-Motive Marriages: What's Next for Buyer-Seller Relations?" *Sloan Management Review,* Spring 1990, pp. 29–35.

McAdams, J., and Hawk, E. *Capitalizing on Human Assets, The Benchmark Study.* Phoenix: American Compensation Association; Houston: American Quality and Productivity Center, 1992.

McClenahen, J. C. "Not Fun in the Sun." *Industry Week,* Oct. 15, 1990, pp. 22–24.

McCorcle, M. D. "Critical Issues in the Functioning of Interdisciplinary Groups." *Small Group Behavior,* Aug. 1982, 13(3), 291–310.

McKeown, J. J. "New Products from New Technologies." *Journal of Business and Industrial Marketing,* Winter-Spring 1990, pp. 67–72.

Miller, C. "How to Construct Programs for Teams." *Reward and Recognition* (Supplement to *Training*), Sept. 1991, pp. 4–6.

Mower, J., and Wilemon, D. "Rewarding Technical Teamwork." *Research-Technology Management*, Sept.-Oct. 1989, pp. 24–29.

Murray, T. "Team Selling: What's the Incentive?" *Sales and Marketing Management*, June 1991, pp. 89–92.

Norman, C. A., and Zawacki, R. A. "Team Appraisal-Team Approach." *Personnel Journal*, Sept. 1991, pp. 101–104.

Nulty, P. "The Soul of an Old Machine." *Fortune*, May 21, 1990, pp. 67–72.

O'Dell, C. "Team Play, Team Pay—New Ways of Keeping Score." *Across the Board*, Nov. 1989, pp. 38–45.

O'Dell, C., and McAdams, J. *People, Performance and Pay.* Phoenix: American Compensation Association; Houston: American Quality and Productivity Center, 1987.

Opper, S. "Groupware: Technology Makes Teamwork Easier." *Trial*, Jan. 1990, pp. 49–51.

"Organizational, Individual Factors Pose Biggest Barriers for Teams." *Total Quality*, Dec. 1992, p. 5.

Orsburn, J. D., Moran, L., Musselwhite, E., and Zenger, J. *Self-Directed Work Teams: The Next American Challenge.* Homewood, Ill.: Business One Irwin, 1990.

Parker, G. M. *Team Players and Teamwork: The New Competitive Business Strategy.* San Francisco: Jossey-Bass, 1990.

Parker, G. M. *Parker Team Player Survey.* Tuxedo, N.Y.: Xicom, 1991.

Parker, G. M. "Getting into Shape." *Managing Service Quality*, July 1992, pp. 251–254.

Parker, G. M., and Kropp, R. P., Jr. *50 Activities for Self-Directed Teams.* Amherst, Mass.: HRD Press, 1994.

Parker, G. M., and Kropp, R. P., Jr. *50 Activities for Team Building.* Amherst, Mass.: HRD Press, 1992.

Pearson, P. H. "The Interdisciplinary Team Process, or the Professionals of Babel." *Developmental Medicine and Child Neurology*, June 1983, pp. 390–395.

Penzer, E. "A Philadelphia Story." *Incentive*, July 1991, pp. 33–36.

Phillips, S. L., and Elledge, R. L. *The Team-Building Source-book*. San Diego, Calif.: University Associates, 1989.

Reddy, W. B. (ed.). *Team Building: Blueprints for Productivity and Satisfaction*. Alexandria, Va.: NTL Institute for Applied Behavioral Science; San Diego, Calif.: University Associates, 1988.

Renzulli, J. S., Owen, S. V., and Callahan, C. M. "Fluency, Flexibility and Originality as a Function of Group Size." *Journal of Creative Behavior*, 1974, 8, 107–112.

Robinson, R., Oswald, S. L., Swinehart, K. S., and Thomas, J. "Southwest Industries: Creating High-Performance Teams for High-Technology Production." *Planning Review*, Nov.-Dec. 1991, pp. 10–14, 47.

Sato, K. "Trust and Group Size in a Social Dilemma." *Japanese Psychological Research*, 1988, 30, 88–93.

Sellers, P. "How to Remake Your Sales Force." *Fortune*, May 4, 1992, pp. 96–103.

Senge, P. M. "The Leader's New Work: Building Learning Organizations." *Harvard Business Review*, Fall 1990, pp. 7–23.

Sherman, S. "A Brave New Darwinian Workplace." *Fortune*, Jan. 25, 1993, pp. 50–56.

"Shifting the Corporate Culture." *Working Woman*, Nov. 1992, pp. 25, 28.

Shonk, J. H. *Team-Based Organizations*. Homewood, Ill.: Business One Irwin, 1992.

Sisco, R. "Put Your Money Where Your Teams Are." *Training*, July 1992, pp. 41–45.

Stratton, A. D. "StorageTek and Excellence Through Quality." *Journal for Quality and Productivity*, Dec. 1991, pp. 6–9.

Thomas, K. W., and Kilmann, R. H. *Thomas-Kilmann Conflict Mode Instrument*. Tuxedo, N.Y.: Xicom, 1974.

The 3M Meeting Management Team. *How to Run Better Business Meetings*. New York: McGraw-Hill, 1979.

Torres, C., and Spiegel, J. *Self-Directed Work Teams: A Primer*. San Diego, Calif.: Pfeiffer, 1990.

Vasilash, G. S. "Chrysler Gets Serious About Success." *Production*, Jan. 1992, pp. 58–60.

"Vendor Certification Improves Buyer/Seller Relationships." *Total Quality*, May 1990, pp. 1-3.

Vogt, J. F., and Murrell, K. L. *Empowerment in Organizations.* San Diego, Calif.: University Associates, 1990.

Wallace, R., and Halverson, W. "Project Management: A Critical Success Factor or a Management Fad?" *Industrial Engineering*, Apr. 1992, pp. 48-50.

Wellins, R. S., Byham, W. C., and Wilson, J. M. *Empowered Teams: Creating Self-Directed Work Groups That Improve Quality, Productivity, and Participation.* San Francisco: Jossey-Bass, 1991.

White, M. "Linking Compensation to Knowledge Will Pay Off in the 1990s." *Planning Review*, Nov.-Dec. 1991, pp. 15-17.

Whiting, R. "Core Teams Take the Front Lines." *Electronic Business*, June 17, 1991, pp. 50-54.

Wolff, M. F. "Teams Speed Commercialization of R&D Projects." *Research-Technology Management*, Sept.-Oct. 1988, pp. 8-10.

I N D E X

Differentiation, in groups, 98
Digital Equipment Corporation
    (DEC), Colorado Springs,
    Colorado, 110
Doherty, E. M., 124–125
Dotlich, D., 107–108
Dowler, T., 16
Doyle, M., 37, 145
Draden, G., 152
Dumaine, B., 10, 22, 67, 69, 83
Dyer, W., 207

E

Eastman Chemical, 111
Edwards, M. R., 107, 111
Eisman, R., 126, 134
Elliott, V., 126
Employee-based recognition
    programs, 127–129
Empowered Manager, The, 208
Empowered Teams, 208
Empowerment in Organizations,
    208
Empowerment, 47–48, 58, 66–79;
    impacting factors in, 73–74;
    methods of, 70–73; real-time,
    67–70
Evaluation survey, 195–196,
    199–205
External relations. *See* Boundary
    management

F

Feedback, as motivator, 106
Fern, E. F., 152
*50 Activities for Self-Directed
    Teams*, 208
Flexibility, in team leader, 59
Ford Motor Company, 9; Probe
    design, 12
Fried, L., 154
Functional teams, 26–27, 34,
    35, 39

G

Gainsharing, 118–120
General Electric, 124
"Getting Into Shape," 181
Glass, A., 175
Goal(s): assessment, 89; and
    company vision, 48; defined,
    87; and empowerment, 72; and
    false consensus, 165
Goal setting: and conflict
    reduction, 81–82; leadership
    responsibility in, 58–59; and
    partnership building, 82–83;
    techniques, 83–85
*Goal Setting: A Motivational
    Technique That Works*, 209
Gomez-Meija, L. R., 133
Gordon, J., 32, 33
Government agencies, cross-
    functional teamwork in, 15, 29
Group dynamics, 178
Group process skills, 57–60
Groups, versus teams, 34–35
Gupta, Y. P., 9, 38, 94

H

Hackman, J. R., 152
Halverson, W., 7, 26, 172
Handy, C., 209
Hanley, J., 10, 68
Hare, M., 152
Hastings, C., 45, 90, 208
Hawk, E., 119, 125, 209
Health care industry, team-selling
    approach in, 18–19
Henke, J. W., 70
Henkoff, R., 16, 28
Hewlett-Packard, 108
Higginbotham, A., 157
High-tech industries, cross-
    functional team selling in,
    20–21
Hills, C. H., 20, 21, 22, 142
Hines, W., 70–71, 72, 75, 109, 156
Hoerr, J., 69
Hoffman La Roche, 38